*Write on a scroll what you see
and send it to the seven churches: to
Ephesus,
Smyrna,
Pergamum,
Thyateira,
Sardis,
Philadelphia,
and Laodicea.
(Rv 1:11)*

a guide to
THE SEVEN CHURCHES
Fatih Cimok

A TURİZM YAYINLARI

FRONT COVER
Church M in Sardis with
the Temple of Artemis.

BACK COVER
Map of western Anatolia
showing the Seven Churches.

HALF-TITLE PAGE
Painting of St John the
Theologian. The Dark Church. Mid-eleventh
century. Göreme Outdoor Museum. Cappadocia.

PICTURES
Archives of A Turizm Yayınları

First printing March 1998
Third printing July 1999

ISBN 975-7199-66-4

PUBLISHERS
A Turizm Yayınları Ltd Şti
Şifa Hamamı Sokak 18,
34400 Sultanahmet, İstanbul, Turkey
Tel: (0212) 516 24 97 Fax: (0212) 516 41 65

CONTENTS

The fifth scourge from the Revelation. Detail from a manuscript (974) from the archives of the Cathedral of Girona, Spain. Revelation 9:7-10 reads: *The appearance of the locusts was like that of horses ready for battle. On their heads they wore what looked like crowns of gold; their faces were like human faces, and they had hair like women's hair. Their teeth were like lions' teeth, and they had chests like iron breastplates. The sound of their wings was like the sound of many horse-drawn chariots racing into battle. They had tails like scorpions, with stingers; with their tails they had power to harm people for five months.*

INTRODUCTION

The subject of this book is the letters written to the Seven Churches of Asia Minor in the book of Revelation by St John of Patmos, also known as St John the Theologian, or the Divine. It is prepared by a former tour guide who has visited the destinations of these letters so often and with so many travellers, that the way in which the subject is treated may appeal to the general reader more than a book which may have been written by a professional archaeologist, historian or cleric.

The 'Revelation' or 'Apocalypse' of St John, the last book of the Bible, is probably the most difficult to understand because of its symbolic language. It is a typical example of a type of literature known as apocalyptic, namely pertaining to the revelation of secret matters connected with the end of the world. As a result of successive Jewish failures between the third century BCE and the first century CE to establish a just and prosperous kingdom, there were increased eschalogical hopes and expectations, hence the popularity of apocalyptic literature. The book of Daniel, which was written in the second century BCE to encourage the Jews who suffered under the oppression inflicted by the Seleucid king Antiochus IV Epiphanes (175-164 BCE) on which St John draws often, is the best known example of this type of literature.

As there has been little excavation in some of these cities, not much is known about the material culture of their early Christian phases. At those sites where excavations have revealed traces of many church buildings, none is older than the mid-fourth century, probably dating from the reign of the Byzantine emperor Constantius (337-61), son of Constantine the Great. In any case, there is little chance of encountering church building of this early period, as the Christians are thought to have met and prayed in large houses, synagogues, grottos or outdoors.

Following the introductory historical background of the region, the relevant details are briefly repeated in the history of each city. The Turkish equivalent of names and the reign of rulers are usually mentioned in parentheses when they are used for the first time. All biblical quotations are from the New American Bible, 1987 edition, Nashville, USA and in italics. The dates which are not marked as BCE (BC) or Before Common Era are Common Era, CE (AD).

Gold jewellery from Troia II (about 2600-2450 BCE). İstanbul Archaeological Museum.

HISTORICAL BACKGROUND

Asia Minor or Anatolia[1] is a large peninsula which protrudes like a bridgehead from Asia towards Europe. The centre of this peninsula is a vast undulating plateau. The Pontic mountains of the north and the Taurus range in the south, prevent this high plateau from receiving any rain except for a short winter period. Along the Mediterranean and Black Sea coasts, deep and narrow bays where ships can take shelter are rare. The east of the peninsula is covered with high mountains: Mt Ararat (5,165 metres), legendary resting place of Noah's ark, still sought by some, is the highest. Here, between high mountains, the tributaries of two of the rivers of Eden, the Tigris and Euphrates flow.

In the west of the peninsula the landscape changes. It is to this different geography that western Anatolia, 'Asia'[2] of the Romans, owes its unique cultural and historical development. Here, the short mountain ranges run at right angles to the sea and allow the rain clouds to reach inland; in the low valleys which extend between worn out heights, are rivers fed by the snow of mountain peaks in

[1] From Greek *anatole* which means east.

[2] It has been claimed that the word derives from *Assuwa* which is thought to be the name of the region in the Hittite texts.

Gold figurine of a woman from the Temple of Artemis in Ephesus. End of the seventh-beginning of the sixth centuries BCE. Efes Archaeological Museum. Selçuk.

the spring and dry most of the summer. The Caicus (Bakırçay), Hermus (Gediz), Cayster (Küçük Menderes) and Meander (Büyük Menderes) are the most important of these rivers. The latter has come to mean the word which so well describes its undulating progress to the sea.

The soil is fertile and the region produces a substantial portion of Turkey's cotton and tobacco. The low mountain slopes are covered with vineyards and orchards of figs, pomegranates and many other kinds of fruit. Olive oil and wine have been two of the region's main produce since antiquity. The jagged coastline creates hundreds of deep inlets protected from the Aegean wind, where harbours could be built easily. Excavations have shown that the western coast of Anatolia was thickly populated during the late Bronze Age (about 1500-1200 BCE). Some of these settlements such as Troia and ancient Smyrna (Bayraklı) have shown continuous occupation, beginning in the third millennium and extending to the historical period.

Around 1200 BCE, the tranquil picture of the region suddenly changed. Nomadic marauders later named the Sea People, overran the Aegean islands, Anatolia, Cyprus and Syria as far as Egypt. According to Egyptian texts, nothing could stand against these hordes. Their arrival is generally linked to the end of Mycenean kingdom in Greece, and the Hittites in Anatolia. By the ninth-eighth centuries BCE the ancient pattern of society had vanished. On the ruins of the destroyed or abandoned cities small villages or strongholds rose. Little has survived of these centuries, sometimes referred to as 'Dark Ages', a state which describes our lack of knowledge.

The Greek colonization of the Aegean shores of Anatolia is thought to have begun as early as the eleventh century and continued with intervals until the seventh century BCE. The first waves brought the Aeolians to the region north of Smyrna, Dorians to Caria, Rhodes and Cos and Ionians to the area between the two.

The new immigrants settled along the Aegean coastline close to the river mouths. Deep and narrow inlets enabled them to build harbours where their fishing fleets and merchant vessels could shelter. On top of rocky heights, surrounded by good land, farming settlements enclosed in sun-dried brick fortifications on stone foundations were established.

Literary sources suggest and excavations seem to bear out that these settlements, initially small villages and ruled by hereditary kings, had become independent city-states with a kind of primitive democracy by the seventh and sixth centuries BCE. Miletus, Ephesus, Assos, Priene, Phocaea, and Erythrae were among the most important.

Each of these cities (poleis) was governed by institutions created by its citizens. In a city (polis), the people (demos) chose the assembly (ekklesia), which in turn chose the council (boule). The latter governed the city in the name of the people. Being a member of such a polis became an important characteristic of this settled society, distinguishing it from the world of non-Greeks, regarded as 'uncivilized' or 'Barbarian'.

In the course of time immigrants carried the model elsewhere. Massalia (Marseilles) on the Mediterranean, Cyzicus (Erdek) on the Marmara and Trapezus (Trabzon) on the Black Sea were a few of the colonies established.[3] At the beginning of the seventh century BCE this steady development in western Anatolia was temporarily halted by the Cimmerian hordes who invaded Anatolia from the east. Gordion, capital of the Phrygian kingdom, Sardis, the Lydian capital, Ephesus, and other coastal cities were sacked. Before long this invasion subsided and with the exception of Gordion, the cities recovered.

These Ionian Greek cities were influenced both by local indigenous people and by contacts with their Eastern neighbours. This rich cultural amalgam resulted in a distinctive artistic style which is sometimes referred to as 'East Greek'. Herodotus, Homer, Hippodamus, Thales, Anaximenes, Anaximander and Heraclitus are some of the names belonging to this great flowering of Eastern Greek civilization.

---

[3] In addition to their prowess in sailing, the powerful Lydian and Phrygian kingdoms did not permit the Greeks to expand in the eastern direction.

Royal Persian figure standing on eagle heads. Detail from the relief decoration of a silver and gold Lydian phial. c late sixth century BCE. Uşak Archaeological Museum.

These rich cities of western Anatolia had close contacts with the Lydian kingdom of the hinterland. The latter regarded the Ionian cities as being in its back garden and from time to time interfered with their internal affairs. In 546 BCE the Persians invaded Anatolia, and by the end of the century the whole peninsula was captured and divided into Persian provinces (satrapies). This was one of the major encounters between the Greek world and the East. The cities of Ionia were ruled from the satrapy which was established in Sardis. Lenient treatment of the nations under their rule, leaving them free in their domestic affairs, was the policy of the Persians. Under their new rulers the Ionian cities of western Anatolia kept their autonomous structure and continued to prosper.

The Royal Road which connected Ephesus and Sardis to the Persian capital Susa, altogether some 2,300 kilometres and a trip of ninety days by walking, enabled the Ionian masons, artisans and smiths to travel to the east and work on the projects of Persian rulers. This road, whose origin probably extended to the Hittite period, was the first highway in history which had regularly spaced post houses and inns at about twenty-five kilometre intervals depending on the terrain, with forts and ferries to cross rivers. Now the precious products of the East could be carried faster and more safely. Along with wheeled carts, camel caravans and mule or donkey trains, various beliefs, cults, religions and artistic forms also travelled. Later, early Christian communities would emerge

Personification of the Roman province of Asia. Mosaic. Detail. Museum of El Djem. Tunisia. Second century CE.

at cities founded on the network of such communication and trade routes.

In 334 BCE, Alexander the Great crossed the Dardanelles (Hellespont) and marched into Anatolia. The cities of western Anatolia with the exception of Halicarnassus, which remained loyal to Persia for another hundred and forty years, were thus supposedly liberated from the Persian yoke and gained new momentum and continued to flourish during the long Hellenistic period which followed the death of Alexander.

Urban centres such as Tralles, Magnesia on the Meander, Nyssa or Metropolis gained a new vigour and prospered. With the beginning of the Hellenistic period the centre of commercial and artistic activity had shifted from Greece to Anatolia, Syria and Egypt. New temples, theatres, libraries, colonnaded stoas, gymnasiums and other types of public buildings, often of local stone, were constructed. The masons, carpenters, painters or potters of the West moved to Anatolia, Syria and Egypt to find work in the daring projects begun by the rich and cultivated rulers of the Hellenistic capitals such as the Attalid Pergamum, Seleucid Antioch-on-the-Orontes and Ptolemaic Alexandria. Men of letters and scientists found homes in the libraries of the Hellenistic kings. The spread of Greek as the common language of communication, administration and culture — even it did not reach the rural population — brought this world closer together.

By the time of the early Christians, Anatolia was divided into several Roman provinces. The western part, known as Asia, was governed by proconsuls[4] appointed for one year. The governor proconsul of Asia resided in Ephesus. It was to the benefit of Rome to see that these urban settlements grew and prospered because they were the most important tax sources of the Roman economy. With the beginning of the Imperial Roman period towards the end of the first century BCE, economic exploitation of western Anatolia was replaced by a more careful and relatively just administration and its cities became important sources of income for Rome.

Its location at the centre of the empire, away from frontier crises, enabled this region enjoy the permanent Roman peace (*Pax Romana*) longer than other provinces and gave a chance to the landed aristocracy to control larger areas of land and establish farms outside big cit-

[4] *pro consule* or 'Acting Consul'. One who, not holding the office, exercised consular authority outside Rome by consular appointment.

ies. Agriculture which had survived along with the nomadic animal husbandry gained importance. The demand in the cities encouraged small farming units to work harder and enabled them to turn their produce into currency. The abundance of copper coins among the ru-ins of the ancient sites of western Anatolia points to the widespread use of coinage. New roads were built, bandits were cleared from the land and pirates from the sea. Urban life flourished. People constantly travelled for business or pleasure or for both. For the notables spending money became a virtue. The easiest and shortest way to fame for the rich was by winning the gratitude of multitudes and they began to spend their surplus cash for the 'home town'. The latter would show its gratitude by erecting a statue or giving the person an honorific title. Some undertook the responsibility of meeting the expense of heating the baths. Others paid for singers or dancers during festivals or established wild beast fights or gladiatorial games. However, none of these was as long lasting as building monuments and the educated rich built fountains or libraries. Those who cared more for the sentiment of the lower classes perhaps preferred building baths or stadia. Nevertheless, this willing act of generosity in the course of time came to be seen as a duty by the cities and each display of wealth left the benefactor less rich than before. The first three hundred years of the Common Era was a period of unusual peace and prosperity — albeit enjoyed largely by the upper classes. St John left Palestine and travelled to Ephesus during the beginning of this era.

The great plagues of 165 and 251, each killing about a third of the population, were not enough to interrupt this steady development. Although the region suffered from the invasion of the Goths in the middle of the second century it recovered quickly.[5] The raids of the Sassanians in the early seventh and the Arabs in the seventh and eighth centuries, however, had disastrous effects and brought back the chaos of the 'Dark Ages'. The Sassanian interlude occupied the first quarter of the seventh century. Before Anatolia recovered from its devastation the Arabs' raids began. The latter were to last longer and were more disastrous. Cities and countryside suffered depopulation; people left their homes and migrated to more secure regions; land was left uncultivated; artisans were unable to sell their products and the economy collapsed. On the ruins of the ancient cities there arose hastily built small fortresses. The scarcity of coins and sherds of good quality pottery among the findings of the ruins of this era is not surprising.

Although some of the cities recovered temporarily, the golden age of Late Roman and Early Byzantine Anatolia had come to an end. Thereafter, the region became a battle ground between the Byzantines and the Turkish Emirates, and was even for a short period ruled by Timur. At the beginning of the fifteenth century the Ottomans incorporated the region in their growing empire.

[5] When one of their major human sources which was Anatolia was crippled, Roman emperors began recruiting barbarian hordes from the north of the Danube in their legions.

ST JOHN OF PATMOS

Knowledge of the life of St John of Patmos (also known as the 'Theologian' or the 'Divine'), the author of the book of Revelation, which includes the letters to the Seven Churches of Asia Minor, mostly comes from apochryphal stories recorded after his death.[1] Christian tradition identifies him with other New Testament figures of the same name, St John the Evangelist, the traditional author of the Fourth Gospel who is also claimed to be St John the Apostle. The accounts of the Gospels agree that the latter is the son of Zebedee; together with his brother James (the Greater), he decided to follow Christ while fishing in the Lake Galilee. He became one of Christ's closest disciples and is said to have been with him on various significant occasions such as the Transfiguration and the Crucifixion. According to the Fourth Gospel, also known as the Gospel of John (Jn 19:26-27), on the cross:

> When Jesus saw his mother and the disciple there whom he loved, he said to his mother, 'Woman, behold, your son.' Then he said to the disciple, 'Behold, your mother.' And from that hour the disciple took her into his home.

The disciple *whom he loved*[2] is thought to have been St John. He is said to have been martyred like his brother St James and buried in Jerusalem. Another tradition holds that taking the Virgin with him, St John travelled to Ephesus in Asia Minor, was exiled to the island of Patmos, wrote the Fourth Gospel and the book of Revelation there and finally returned to Ephesus where he died and was buried.

The second half of the first century was full of disasters for the early Christians. The Romans at first regarded Christianity as a new Jewish movement. Like the others it was expected to disappear or survive as a sect after the crucifixion of Christ. When this did not happen and Christians began to challenge (probably not in quantity but in essence) the accepted doctrine of the Synagogue and Rome, its leaders were caught and eliminated.

St Stephen and St James the Less (the traditional brother of Christ) were stoned to death and St James the Greater put to the sword. Sts Peter and Paul were taken to Rome and executed. Many believers had to leave Palestine and seek shelter in other countries. It is during this period, probably during the Jewish Revolt (66-70) which ended with the destruction of the Second Temple in Jerusalem that St John, taking the Virgin with him, travelled to Ephesus.

At that time Ephesus probably had a population of over hundred and fifty thousand, which must have included a large number of Jews, and about a thousand or more Jewish and Gentile Christians. Following the Jewish Revolt, Jews and Jewish Christians of the diaspora[3] began to lose their favourable position in Roman eyes and fall

---

[1] The major source is the apochryphal 'Acts of John' thought to have been recorded in the second century.

[2] Some modern scholars believe that 'the disciple there whom he loved' may refer to all the disciples Christ loved and therefore the entire Church.

[3] The dispersion of the Jews outside the land of Israel

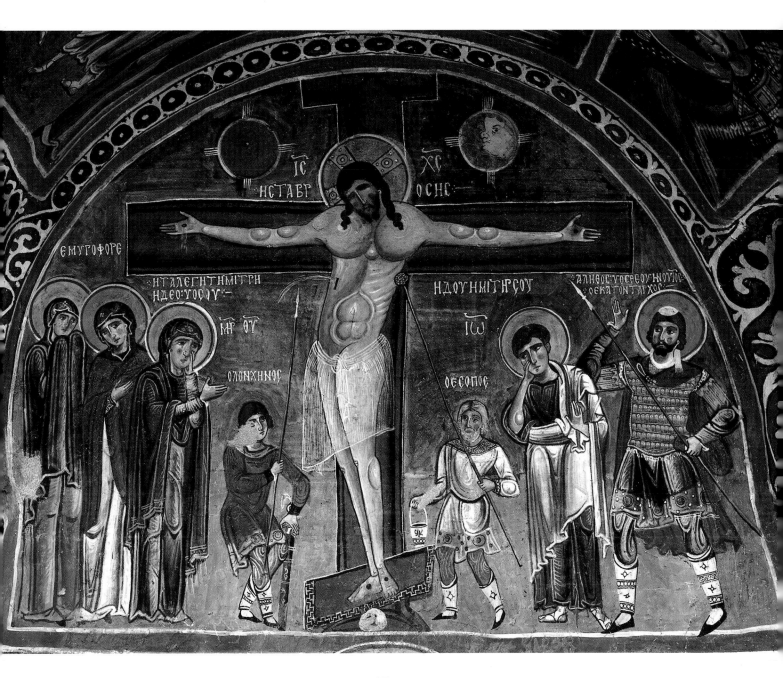

into disgrace. To the discontent of the Jews, the Gentile Christians, since they had not participated in the revolt, were treated better. However by this time the solid Christian communities established during the first missionary wave had been weakened by dissensions and declining numbers. On arriving in Ephesus, St John was shocked to see how some Christians had compromised with pagan practices, a situation which he refers to in his first letter of the Revelation. This is addressed to the Christians in Ephesus.

The first part of the major ancient source which is thought to have narrated the arrival and first stay of St John in Ephesus is lost. What survives relates mostly to his return from Patmos exile; how he began proclaiming the Gospel in Ephesus, his contests with both pagans and heretics among his own community, his miracles and his death there.

In the book of Revelation St John does not give any detailed information about the cause of his exile. He merely says that he was exiled to Patmos on account of the word of God and the testimony of Christ (Rv 1:9). Preaching was not a capital crime which would lead to banishment. As long as they did not cause disturbances the Roman adminstration allowed the people under their rule to worship whatever god or cult they chose. Christians were not regarded as criminals in Roman eyes but members of an illicit religion.

When he was serving as the governor of the province of Bithynia, the younger Pliny wrote to Trajan asking the emperor's advice on what to do with the Christians whose numbers kept on increasing. The governor admitted that although he executed Christians as his predecessors had done, he did not know the exact nature of their crime. Pliny's letter is the first documented account of Christian presence in Anatolia. Trajan, although in the course of time he changed his opinion, did not regard the Christians as dangerous.

In Ephesus it is probable that St John was accused of being an agitator. Being the most prominent figure of his group he might have been chosen to serve as an example. The worst punishment reserved for criminals not sentenced to death, was to strip them of their civil rights and material possessions and banish them to a remote corner of the empire or to an isolated spot. If St John had been accused of refusing to sacrifice to the imperial cult, especially the cult of Domitian (81-96) which was then established in Ephesus, this would have been a capital crime punishable by death. The huge edifice to the south of the state agora in Ephesus was the first temple of the imperial cult erected in Anatolia and its impact must have been on the Christians in this city.

A late Greek tradition has it that after arriving in Ephesus the story of St John's miracles reached the ears of Domitian and he was called to Rome. Here his power was tested in front of the emperor by making him drink a cup of poison which killed a criminal but did not harm him, and by asking him to raise a girl who had supposedly been slain by an evil spirit. Domitian, impressed by what he had witnessed, decided only to banish him to Patmos. His banishment lasted until the death of the emperor.

A tradition popular only among Latin authors, relates that St John was first taken to Rome as prisoner upon the order of the emperor and cast into a cauldron of hot oil[4] at the Latin Gate (the origin of the feast of St John 'Port Latin' or at the 'Latin Gate,' May 6), but he came out unscathed.

The place chosen to banish St John was one of the volcanic islands scattered in the Aegean about eighty kilometres south of Ephesus, and was used as a penal colony. A later Byzantine chronicle refers to the island as

[4] A version of 'Acts of John' claims that the event took place in Ephesus.

Colossal head of the emperor Domitian from his temple in Ephesus. Efes Archaeological Museum. Selçuk.

being 'deserted and uncultivated, covered with and made impassable by thorns and shrubs, and by reason of its aridity completely barren'.

St John was exiled to Patmos together with his young disciple Prochorus, one of the deacons of the Jerusalem church (Acts 6:5). On the way to Patmos he rescued a boy who fell from the ship into the sea. The length of his exile is claimed to have been one and half, or five or fifteen years. During his stay there he did not stop preaching the Gospel and converting the inhabitants. A tradition has it that when his activity was heard at the Temple of Apollo, the priests asked help from a famous magician called Kynops whose most popular trick was to jump into the sea and come out after a while, unharmed. In front of the witnesses challenging St John, he did the same. St John extended his arms in the form of a cross and prayed 'O Thou, who didst grant to Moses by this similitude to over-throw the Amalek,[5] O Lord Jesus Christ, bring down Kynops to the deep of the sea; let him never more behold this sun, nor converse with living men'. After a short while the pet-rified body of the magician surfaced as a rock on the wa-ter a short distance away. The local fishermen claim that to this day the bad taste of the shellfish caught around the rock derives from this magician.

On Patmos St John was unchained and free to go wher-ever he wished. It was in a grotto on Patmos that he wrote the Fourth Gospel and received the visions of the last book of the New Testament known as the book of Rev-elation. Some of the imagery, for instance:

> *Then the sky was divided like a torn*
> *scroll curling up, and every mountain*

[5] The people of southern Palestine and the Sinai peninsula whom the Hebrews encountered after coming out of Egypt. During the war with them 'As long as Moses kept his hands raised up, Israel won (Ex 17:11). Later Moses' outstretched arms were regarded as the prefiguration of the cross.

and island was moved from its place
(Rv 6:14)

or

*Every island fled, and mountains dis-
appeared*
(Rv 16:20)

is thought to have been inspired by the island.

The book of Revelation gives few facts about St John's life, except for the fact that he had a Jewish background and probably a priestly ancestry. So far as is known, he remained celibate. In art he is often shown as an old man on Patmos, seated and writing his book, standing or sitting in front of a cave and looking up into heaven, and writing or dictating to his disciple Prochorus. Sometimes he is shown sitting alone writing the Fourth Gospel. In such representations the inscription on the Gospel or open scroll in his hand or in front of his disciple Prochorus reads *In the beginning was the Word* (Jn 1:1). His attribute is an eagle, because his words carry the reader up to heaven and paper, ink, and a scroll are the common accessories of such compositions.

St John's Patmos exile terminated with Domitian's death. However, his ship was wrecked on leaving Patmos and swimming on a cork St John landed at Miletus; from there he went to Ephesus. Afterwards he is said to have governed the churches in Asia and given advice to their elders until his death in the reign of Trajan (98-117). The apochrypal tradition mentions that one day while preaching in the Temple of Artemis, the altar and other objects in the temple and half of the temple itself, collapsed. Once he was challenged by Aristodemus, high priest of the Temple of Artemis, the Roman Diana, to show the superiority of the Christians' God by drinking out of a poisoned cup. When St John made the sign of cross over the cup, the poison emerged in the shape of a serpent, and he drained the vessel. St John also restored to life

Detail from an eighteenth-century Russian icon showing St John rescuing a young man who fell into the sea on the way to Patmos. Gübelin Edward, Lausanne.

18

Detail from an eighteenth-century Russian icon. St John is saved after the shipwreck. Prochorus is represented ashore. Gübelin Edward, Lausanne.

two criminals under sentence of death who had been made to test beforehand the result of the poison. Having witnessed the miracle both Aristodemus and the proconsul of Ephesus are said to have accepted Christian faith. Among the other miracles he is said to have performed in Ephesus was the raising of Drusiana, a widow with whom he had lodged before he was exiled to Patmos. As her funeral passed by she sat up in her coffin at St John's command and went home to prepare a meal for him. During his residence in Ephesus he is claimed to have gone to Smyrna where he won St Polycarp to Christianity and made him the bishop of the city.

Another tradition claims that during his last years St John built a hut on the isolated Ayasuluk hill and lived there and wrote the fourth book of the New Testament known by his name.

He is thought to have died at a great age, claimed to have been a hundred and twenty, around the year 100 and to be buried on the hill. This may be the reason why he is sometimes depicted as a very old man with a long white beard, even when he is in the early years of his life in Palestine.

According to tradition, after his tomb was dug, he laid himself down in it and gave up his spirit. The following day his body was not found because presumably he had ascended to heaven. Another tradition claims that only his sandals were found and the earth over his grave was moving as if stirred by his breathing. The Latin tradition has it that after his prayer there appeared over him a great light at which no one could look; then he laid himself down and gave up his ghost. Immediately manna[6] issued from his tomb and continued issuing forth. By the end of the second century most of the churches in western Anatolia regarded him as their founder.

[6] Divinely supplied spiritual nourishment.

LETTERS TO THE CHURCHES OF ASIA

The book of Revelation[1] consists of letters addressed to the Seven[2] Churches in Asia Minor and visions of the final cosmic conflict between the forces of the Satan and God's angels which ends with the victory of the latter.

The letters to the Seven Churches form a small portion of the book at the beginning. Their form may have been inspired by the letters of St Paul. They are artificial letters or parts of a particular letter which bears a single message. They are written not to be read but to be preached. They are regarded as having been written to be read together for the purpose of encouraging the reader to remain loyal to his faith and to provide him with comfort and warn him about the catastrophic events described afterwards.

The letters begin with similar addresses and end in identical expressions. In his first vision St John is commanded to write what he sees to the Seven Churches:

> I, John, your brother, who share with you the distress, the kingdom, and the endurance we have in Jesus, found myself on the island called Patmos because I proclaimed God's word and

[1] Greek *Apocalypse*, from the verb *apocalyptein*, to 'uncover' or 'reveal'

[2] It is the most frequently used number in Christian literature and chosen by St John to refer to the universal church. It is also the most popular epic cliché in ancient literature, such as the six day of rain followed by the seventh day when it stopped (Babylonian Deluge) or the six days of creation and the seventh day of rest (Genesis).

Dedicatory cross on steps from one of the columns flanking the entrance of the southern aisle of the Church of St John the Theologian. Byzantine period. Selçuk.

gave testimony to Jesus. I was caught up in spirit on the Lord's day and heard behind me a voice as loud as a trumpet, which said, 'Write on a scroll what you see and send it to the seven churches: to Ephesus, Smyrna, Pergamum, Thyateira, Sardis, Philadelphia, and Laodicea.'

(Rv 1:9-11)

The vision appears to St John on the Lord's day, that is Sunday and with a loud voice accompanying it. The loud voice is a common motif of the eschatological visions in the Old Testament. He attributes his inspiration and visions to the *spirit* and writes at its dictation. This is the Spirit of God. In the biblical narratives a trumpet call announces a divine judgement. By the church (Greek *ekklesia*) St John meant the Christian community which existed in each of these cities. In choosing the Seven Churches he is thought to have preferred those with which he was more familiar and which were established on the popular communication routes. What is common to all of them is that they were flourishing Roman towns with Christian communities, which had probably developed in their Hellenized Jewish communities.

By the time St John came to western Anatolia Christianity had existed for a generation and the promised Second Coming, Christ's appearance which would announce the Last Judgement, had not occurred. After so many years the Christians of the time must have looked back and probably realized that neither had their size increased nor their material conditions improved.[3] In a city like Ephesus for instance, where there must have been over a dozen sects or cults, theirs was probably still one of the smallest. In almost all of these cities there were members of the Christian community who compromised with the prevailing religious atmosphere and there were signs of weakness and disappointment. During his long stay on Patmos St John must have found time to reflect on the problems threatening Christianity and decided to write the book of Revelation and thus remind Christians of the punishment and rewards of the impending Second Coming and that they must wait and endure for longer.

St John continues:

> *Then I turned to see whose voice it was that spoke to me, and when I turned, I saw seven gold lampstands[4] and in the midst of the lampstands one like a son of man, wearing an ankle-length robe, with a gold sash around his chest. The hair of his head was as white as white wool or as snow and his eyes were like a fiery flame. His feet were like polished brass refined in a furnace, and his voice was like*

[3] Their disappointment brings to mind that of the Jewish population who witnessed the revival of the Persian empire of the fifth century BCE which they had expected to collapse.

[4] The imagery may have been inspired by the seven-branched Jewish lampstand.

The Revelation of St John the Theologian. Icon from Sinop Museum. Nineteenth century. It shows the vision of St John as he recounts at the beginning of the book of Revelation (1:12-20).

the sound of rushing water. In his right hand he held seven stars. A sharp two-edged sword came out of his mouth, and his face shone like the sun at its brightest.

When I caught sight of him, I fell down at his feet as though dead. He touched me with his right hand and said, 'Do not be afraid. I am the first and the last, the one who lives. Once I was dead, but now I am alive forever and ever. I hold the keys to death and the netherworld. Write down, therefore, what you have seen, and what is happening, and what will happen afterwards. This is the secret meaning of the seven stars you saw in my right hand, and of the seven gold lampstands: the seven stars are the angels of the seven churches, and the seven lampstands are the seven churches.

(Rv 1:12-20)

The vision of St John derives from the established literary tradition of visions — mostly from the book of Daniel — which describes God as having superhuman light, beauty or size, all features deriving from Near Eastern pagan images of a god. It is not known for sure whether these visions are real experiences or literary conventions employed by St John.

The seven golden candlesticks represent the Seven Churches. Among them sits *one like a son of man*. The apocalyptic figure *son of man* is also inspired by Daniel 7:13 where he is described as God's representative, who comes surrounded by clouds to bring in the kingdom; but here he is a glorified ruler and judge. The title 'Son of Man' is the most characteristic way of God referring to himself. The figure wears an ankle-length robe and a golden girdle around his chest and crossed over his breast, both marking him as a high priest, the metaphors being selected from the Old Testament. A divine glory envelops him because he is the exalted Christ, the coming Messiah.[5] In his right hand he holds seven stars which symbolize the universal dominion. When St John catches sight of God he falls down on the ground. God introduces himself as *the first and the last, the one who lives*. The image commands St John to write down what he has seen.

The seven stars in his right hand are the angels of the Seven Churches; the angel standing for both the guardian angel and messenger and also the embodiment of the essential characteristics of the churches. These characteristics involve temptations mentioned in his letters, and they may be common to all the churches of his time. Each lampstand represents one of the Christian communities established in one of the seven cities of Asia Minor.

[5] The 'Anointed One'; the Greek *Christos*, the Hebrew word *mashiah* in the Old Testament, means just a sacred person or legitimate ruler and does not identify him with the expected superhuman Messiah.

CHRISTIANITY AND THE IMPERIAL CULT

The roots of the Roman emperor-worship go back to the Hellenistic period. Alexander the Great believed in his divinity during his lifetime and regarded Heracles and thus Zeus as his divine ancestors. This belief was shared by most of his army and his generals. After capturing Egypt he also regarded himself as the son of Amon, the latter being equivalent of Zeus in the Egyptian pantheon. The cities he captured welcomed him as a god and offered sacrifices. His deification began perhaps with the initiation of cities and probably consisted of modest acts such as the offering of the first fruits of the year or holding banquets in his honour on important occasions such as his birthday or succession to the throne, the practices probably going back to the Assyrian world of the second millennium BCE. The participants in such meetings were also limited to a few of privileged people. After his death the Successors who inherited his vast empire did not mind — even encouraged — being treated in the same manner and the practice helped to legitimize their dynasty as rulers. They were regarded as divine during their lifetime and temples or altars were raised for them.

From the city's side the practice enabled it to enjoy material privileges, benefits and prestige, provided by the imperial authority. With the erection of an imperial temple the city gained the title of 'temple-keeper', Greek *neokoros*.[1] From the ruler's point of view the practice con-

firmed his political power and authority.

Even before the power of the Hellenistic kingdoms was completely replaced by that of Rome the cities of western Anatolia began sending envoys to Republican Rome offering its senators to establish their cults, in the Hellenistic manner. Although in some cases the offer was turned down[2] most of the time it was welcomed. Caesar was deified after he was murdered in 44 BCE. Augustus, his adopted son, thus became *divi filius*, 'son of the divine'. After this period the establishment of an imperial cult became an object of competition among cities. The first Roman imperial cult established in Anatolia was that of Augustus (31 BCE-14 CE). By the time that St John wrote the book of Revelation, there was a clearly defined imperial cult and most of the towns in the region had an imperial temple or at least an imperial altar. In his letters to each of the Seven Churches St John gives hints that he was familiar with the detail of the imperial rites practiced in each of them.

The festival held for the imperial cult was the most important event of a city's social activities.[3] It was celebrated at regular or irregular intervals. It was arranged meticulously and carried out with the participancy of the entire

---

[1] The word derives from the Greek *neos*, temple and *koreo*, to sweep. From 'temple sweeper' the word came to mean 'temple-keeper'.

[2] The Roman statesman Cicero mentions his refusal of statues, shrines and chariots offered him when he visited Cyprus in 50 BCE.

[3] The best surviving account of festivals arranged for the imperial cult belongs to Antiochus I of Commagene (69-31 BCE) on Mt Nemrut.

population, each person being obliged to fulfil his duty. During the event the city was crowded with visitors and pilgrims both from neighbouring and remote regions. When the festival was over most of these visitors would stay longer to visit oracles, listen to philosophers, enjoy hot springs or brothels or just for business. Often tents were set at forums to accommodate them. The money they spent on food, lodging, gifts and sacrifices was one of the major incomes of the city. The bakers, tailors, blacksmiths, potters and other artisans made thriving business.

The temples, altars and major civic buildings were adorned with garlands. Images of the emperor and other gods — silver or probably silver overlaid with gold — or ritual objects, were anointed, decorated with wreaths and crowns and afterwards were taken out of the main temples where they were usually kept, and paraded through the main streets on litters borne by men or carts pulled by a pair of horses. These were carried at the front of the procession.[4] The statues included those of the reigning emperor, the image of the founder of the city and local gods and goddesses. As in the course of time immigrants, veteran soldiers and other new arrivals extended the variety of ethnic groups, the number of gods increased. In other words, there was never a shortage of gods or goddesses.

The procession included the imperial priest, chief magistrates of the city, officials, priests and priestesses and corps of young boys (ephebes), all wearing white; sacrificial animals (bulls, pigs, ewes or similar) some bearing signs proclaiming their donors, led by the temple boys or maidens. As the procession passed by their houses, people came out and sacrificed on small altars placed on either side of the main street. Children, peddlers, prostitutes, sightseers and others constituted the tail of this procession. In the absence of weekends or public holidays, such events gave them the chance to forget their everyday life. Money was distributed from public funds so that everybody could afford a sacrifice. The procession continued towards the theatre or stadium or gymnasium, any of the open public assembly places. Here, statues were placed on their pedestals or thrones and sacrifices made on the altars in front of them, incense burned and

[4] In the course of time this was to be imitated by Christians who would carry icons and relics in the same manner.

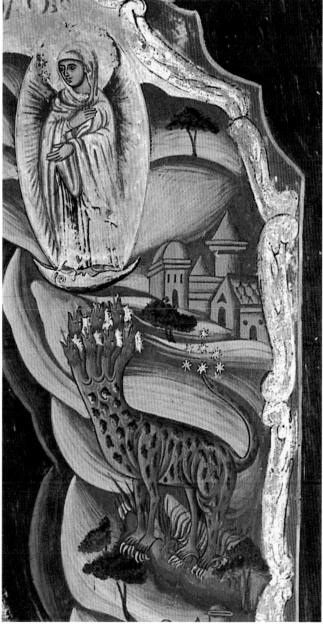

27

libations were poured, cakes and grain were offered and hymns were sung.

The sacrifice was the culminating moment of the festival. It was this pious act which maintained the relations between people and deities. Although its detail varied with locality its basic principles were the same. Often it was carried out by a person who functioned as butcher, cook and sacrificer; a person whose title did not bear any religious significance. The animals such as oxen, sheep or pigs were usually struck down by a blow to the base of the neck. Following skinning the internal parts were separated from the meat. After the prime cuts were offered to the god the sacrificial meat was roasted and banquets were arranged. The prescription of the ancient Greek rituals required the viscera roasted on skewers and eaten by the altar at the beginning by the inner circle of the participants. Some of the meat was boiled in cauldrons and kept for the banquet or to be distributed. The sausages made from the entrails were also regarded as sacrificial food. The priest, king or important officials received the prestigious parts such as thighs, hindquarters, shoulders and tongues. The parts which were offered to the god went to the high priest. The remains were sold in the market.

The ceremony enabled the large numbers of people who could not afford meat to taste it. For Christians the eating of this meat was a kind of communion with a pagan deity. The poorer pagan classes abhorred the refusal of Christians to participate in the sacrifice because it was thought to anger the gods and cause natural disasters. After the sacrifices various sorts of games were arranged. The spectacles included athletic contests, animal fights and gladiatorial combats. Condemned criminals of low status would be burned or thrown to beasts.

The resistance of Christians to the festivities held for the imperial cult was passive. They probably just avoided participating in the celebrations. It is said that St John showed his protest at the cult of Artemis in Ephesus by attending it dressed in black instead of white. Nevertheless, even if their number was not high the withdrawal of Christian citizens from a festival was a worrying fact for the rest of the population, because such processions were reflections of the civic identity of a city. When St John arrived in Ephesus the most bewildering thing for him was the popularity of the imperial cult and the fact that some Christians were actually participating in it.

Pagan tradition was not against the worship of other gods or cults — old or new. So long as it was not reflected on the political stage, pagans did not mind whatever Christians believed and practiced, even if from their point of view eating the flesh and drinking the blood of a god (the Christian Communion or Eucharist) was a sort of cannibalism and as repulsive as the circumcision of Jews. The worship of the Virgin as the Mother of God[5] was something they could understand more easily. In Anatolia the Great Mother had been worshipped for thousands of years under various names such as Kubaba, Cybele, Ma, Anaitis, Artemis or Diana. Pagans may have thought that the Mother of God of the Christians was probably one of the new forms of their already popular Great Mother of many names. The Ephesians had already accorded Isis the same title. However, the refusal

---

[5] Greek *Theotokos* = 'God-bearer'.

of sacrifice for the emperor was something else. It was the refusal of sacrificing to the imperial cult that the local people could not tolerate and caused severe punishments.[6] The reaction was denying divine honour to the emperor and was regarded not just as a religious matter but political subversion. Otherwise, at the time that St John lived in western Anatolia the Christians in any city hardly exceeded one per cent of the total population. In Roman eyes they were not regarded as a threat, and when persecutions of Christians occurred the cause was their refusal to take part in the imperial cult.

Some of the imagery in the book of Revelation is thought to reflect the political world of western Asia Minor at the time St John lived.

In the Revelation the hierarchy of evil forces consists of the dragon (Satan) and the beast to whom it gives its power:

> Then I saw a beast come out of the sea with ten horns and seven heads; on its horns were ten diadems, and on its head blasphemous name[s]. The beast I saw was like a leopard, but it had feet like a bear's, and its mouth was like the mouth of a lion. To it the dragon gave its own power and

throne, along with great authority. I saw that one of its heads seemed to have been mortally wounded, but this mortal wound was healed. Fascinated, the whole world followed after the beast.

> (Rv 13:1-3)

It has been claimed that the beast which St John saw rising from the sea represented the power of Rome which reached Anatolia from the sea. Sometimes the beast is also identified with one of the Roman emperors, Nero, Gaius Caligula or Domitian, who persecuted Christians.

After St John's next vision the meaning of the previous one becomes more clear:

> Then I saw another beast come up out of the earth; it had two horns like a lamb's but spoke like a dragon. It wielded all the authority of the first beast in its sight and made the earth and its inhabitants worship the first beast, whose mortal wound had been healed. It performed great signs, even making fire come down from heaven to earth in the sight of everyone. It deceived the inhabitants of the earth with the signs it was allowed to perform in the sight of the first beast, telling them to make an image for the beast who had been wounded by the

[6] Only Jews were given the right to separate their political obligations from religious ones. They could obey Roman law and worship their own God. Like Christians, however, they were also regarded as 'atheists' — people who refused to worship the gods of Rome.

sword and revived. It was then permitted to breathe life into the beast's image, so that the beast's image could speak and (could) have anyone who did not worship it put to death. It forced all the people, small and great, rich and poor, free and slave, to be given a stamped image on their right hands or their foreheads, so that no one could buy or sell except one who had the stamped image of the beast's name or the number that stood for its name.

Wisdom is needed here; one who understands can calculate the number of the beast, for it is a number that stands for a person. His number is six hundred and sixty-six.

(Rv 13:11-18)

The second beast which came out of the earth is thought to have represented the local authority which served Rome. This authority was represented by the 'proconsul' and the 'Asiarch', the latter holding the title of 'high priest' as well. It was the high priest's responsibility to see that the games and festivals in the *commune Asiae*, or the Asian Confederation, were held properly and emperor-worship carried out with due respect. Since St John was exiled during the reign of Domitian, the metaphor is based probably on the establishment of the cult of Domitian in Ephesus. The temple erected then had a colossal statue, parts of which are in the Efes Archaeological Museum in Selçuk.

This event must have caused great pressure on the Christians and led to persecutions and St John felt it necessary to encourage his flock by sending them messages from where he was banished. In the book of Revelation (Rv 17:6) he refers to Rome as a woman drunk with the blood of Christian believers and saints, who were killed because they had been loyal to Christ. Rome is described as a woman seated on a scarlet beast with seven heads and ten horns (Rv 17:3). The seven heads of the beast were probably inspired by the seven hills of Rome and ten horns may refer to its various emperors.

As far as his image of the beast whose number *stands for a person*, scholars think that this is the only instance in the New Testament where the word 'number' (Greek *arithmos*) assumes a special meaning. St John claims that behind the beast and the number there is however concealed a human figure, known to hearers and readers of the time. The total of the numerical values[7] of the consonants of the Hebrew script for Caesar Nero (*qsr nrwn*) = 100 + 60 + 200 + 50 + 200 + 6 + 50 is 666. The result is thought to refer to the legend that Nero would come back to life and rule again as *Nero redivivus* (restored). This view is accepted by ancient writers as well as by the church fathers and other Christian writers of the later period and the emperor is often thought of as an antichrist. Some thought that Domitian was Nero's reincarnation.

[7] According to number symbolism (gematria) numerical equivalents of letters may be used to understand the concealed meanings of texts.

Marble statue of Androclus, legendary founder of Ephesus, which comes from the Gymnasium of Vedius in Ephesus. Second century. İzmir Archaeological Museum.

ANCIENT EPHESUS

Tradition has it that in the eleventh or tenth century BCE when the first Greek settlers arrived, there were local people living around a temple dedicated to the Anatolian Great Mother, which stood by the sea on the northern slope of Mt Pion. The new arrivals built a city and their own Temple of Artemis, adopting the native goddess under the name of their own; the remains of the Hellenistic temple stand here.

Ephesus' location in the middle of Anatolia's western coast at the point where the main inland route reached the sea, its sheltered harbour at the mouth of the Cayster river and the sanctuary of Artemis which brought pilgrims and business, helped it to flourish.

When the Persians captured Asia Minor, Ephesus was part of Lydia; in 546 BCE it became part of the Persian satrapy established in Sardis. In 496 BCE the city joined the Ionian revolt against Persia and suffered its results. Persian rule lasted until 334 BCE, the arrival of Alexander the Great. As with other cities in the area, except Halicar-nassus, Ephesus opened its gates to Alexander. Twenty-two years earlier in 356 BCE, on the day of Alexander's birth, the Temple of Artemis was destroyed in a fire by a lunatic named Herostratus who wished to make

(opposite) Ruins of the Temple of Hadrian in Ephesus. Beginning of the second century.

his name immortal.[1] Alexander is said to have wanted to rebuild the temple. His offer however was turned down by the Ephesians on the grounds that it was not proper for 'one god to dedicate a temple to another'. The new temple built was considered as one of the seven wonders of the world.

The city of the present day ruins was founded by Lysimachus in about 289 BCE. He was one of Alexander's generals and received western Asia Minor and Thrace during the wars of the Successors. It was built between the small mountains called Coressus (Bülbül Dağı) and Pion (Panayır Dağı) and flourished like the other Hellenistic metropolises of the period. From this period there remains only the fortification on Mt Coressus which catch one's eye during the drive to the house of the Virgin.

When the first Artemis Temple was built, the silting caused by the Cayster river had already made the bay of Ephesus unnavigable for large ships. For this reason Lysimachus moved Ephesus to its present day location. On his death (281 BCE) Ephesus with the rest of western Anatolia became a Seleucid possession.

Excavations show that first three hundred years of the present era was a period of unusual wealth in Ephesus and the rest of western Anatolia. During this period the city became the greatest centre of trade, industry and finance with a population of some two hundred thousand.[2]

In 27 BCE, a few years after the establishment of his cult in Ephesus, Augustus visited the city. When St Paul arrived there in about 53, on his return from his second missionary journey, the city probably had the largest Jewish community in western Anatolia, reaching perhaps some ten thousand people. However, the Ephesians did not show the hospitality that they would extend to St John some ten years later. When St Paul preached that gods made by human hands were not gods at all, a silversmith called Demetrius, who made gifts for the Temple of Artemis, realized that his business was in danger and persuaded his friends to gather in the theatre and protest. Although the riot was calmed by officials, St Paul decided to leave the city.

When Constantine the Great (324-37; sole ruler) adopted Christianity as the state religion the pagan temples and the surviving institutions of Ephesus received a mortal blow. Archaeological research has shown that the

[1] It is said that at this time Artemis was fully occupied bringing Alexander into the world.

[2] Paris and London would reach this number after the fifteenth century.

Detail from a silver coin from Ephesus. First century. Efes Archaeological Museum. Selçuk.

(opposite) Theatre of Ephesus.

images of Artemis were defaced, her statues were destroyed or buried and her name was erased from inscriptions. Pagan frescoes were plastered over or scraped off. Statues were sent to lime kilns or crosses carved on their foreheads on the assumption that they were haunted by demons. Churches were erected from the material of Roman monuments. Nymphaea became baptismal pools and the monuments along the main street were decorated with crosses and Christian inscriptions. Although the city was sacked by Goths in 262, Sassanians in 614 and by the Arabs in the seventh and eighth centuries, it recovered each time. The end of the city was not to be brought about by the enemy, but by the Cayster river.

The history of Ephesus is closely connected with this river. As was the case with the harbour of the previous city, this harbour too despite damming and dredging gradually silted up. By the ninth century Ephesus was an inland city and used Phygela[3] and Scala Nuova (Kuşadası) as its harbours. At this date people began to move to the area of the hill of Ayasuluk. However, the old site continued to be inhabited until the end of the Byzantine period, and only went into oblivion with the Turkish occupation in the fifteenth century.

[3] A bay to the north of Kuşadası situated in front of today's Kuştur Summer Village.

35

To the church in Ephesus

To the angel of the church in Ephesus, write this:

'The one who holds the seven stars in his right hand and walks in the midst of the seven gold lampstands says this: "I know your works, your labor, and your endurance, and that you cannot tolerate the wicked; you have tested those who call themselves apostles but are not, and discovered that they are impostors. Moreover, you have endurance and have suffered for my name, and you have not grown weary. Yet I hold this against you: you have lost the love you had at first. Realize how far you have fallen. Repent, and do the works you did at first. Otherwise, I will come to you and remove your lampstand from its place, unless you repent. But you have this in your favor: you hate the works of the Nicolaitans, which I also hate.

' "Whoever has ears ought to hear what the Spirit says to the churches. To the victor I will give the right to eat from the tree of life that is in the garden of God."

(Rv 2:1-7)

The message of St John to the Ephesians introduces Christ in the same way as does the introduction of the book of Revelation: with the seven stars — the seven angels of the churches — in his right hand and walking, among the seven golden lampstands, the symbol of the Seven Churches. The metaphor confirms that Christ is ever present in each of the churches. The light and lamps are often used in the New Testament for describing the function of disciples of Christ in the world. As the lamp on the candlestick lights up the surrounding darkness, so the disciples are to have an illuminating effect upon their environment.

The expression *I know your works, your labor, and your endurance* is encountered at the beginning of each of his letters and refers to the work and weariness in this world which one day will be over. The Ephesians realized that those who called themselves apostles were nothing but impostors and did not follow them. They have not sinned by following the preaching of liars, that is false teachers. They have suffered for preferring Christ instead of impostors.

Although they accepted their own divinity, until Domitian, the enthusiasm of Roman emperors for the offers of deification and the establishment of their cults outside Rome had been within limits. Until then only Gaius Caligula (37-41) had taken his divinity very seriously.[1] The situation changed with the succession of Domitian (81-96) who wanted to be addressed as 'our Master and our God' (an expression that Christians could only use to refer to Christ) and those who questioned the idea were

[1] Even though they expected people to believe in their own divinity it is known that, generally, the Roman emperors themselves did not take the idea very seriously. As he was dying Vespasian (70-79) is claimed to have chuckled 'Dear me! I must be turning into a god'.

One of the two identical inscriptions from the gate at the end of the Marble Street and below the theatre in Ephesus. In Greek it reads 'Long live the Christian emperors and Greens'.

treated as atheists. The tension that the situation created for Jews and Christians was probably felt strongest in Ephesus where a temple was erected for Domitian. St John probably praises the Ephesian Christians for the persecutions they suffered without growing weary during this period.

The cause of accusation to Ephesian Christians reflects the general situation that the Christians of the time found themselves in: disappointment in the present day conditions of Christianity and falling away from their original love for the new religion. He blames the Ephesian Christians for not maintaining their first love which is always regarded as being the strongest. Nevertheless there is always the chance to awaken before the corruption eats up the whole body; before the light goes out. Their original love can be renewed only by repentance. Otherwise they will be punished.

The Ephesian Christians are complimented for the hatred they have shown for the Nicolaitans. Nicolas, a convert to Judaism in Antioch (Acts 6:5), and one of the seven deacons of Jerusalem in the first century, became the originator of an early heresy which was named after him. His purpose was to achieve a compromise between Christianity and the prevailing social norms of the time,

by reconciling the observance of certain pagan practices, such as the liberty to commit sexual sins, with membership in the Christian community. However, in his letter to Ephesus St John does not explain the nature of the teaching of the Nicolaitans. He is more explicit about them in his letter to the church in Pergamum. Although the word 'Nicolaitan' is not used, St John refers to the same heresy in his letter to the church of Thyateira.

The believer who endures the persecutions, or 'who conquers' will be granted to eat from *the tree of life,* a tree with supernatural qualities. This is the tree of the city of God mentioned towards the end of the book of Revelation:

> *Then the angel showed me the river of life-giving water, sparkling like crystal, flowing from the throne of God and of the Lamb down the middle of its street. On either side of the river grew the tree of life that produces fruit twelve times a year, once each month; the leaves of the trees serve as medicine for the nations.*
>
> (Rv 22:1-2)

Christian Ruins in Ephesus

At the time that St John lived and preached in Ephesus Christians would have been a very small part of the population. Even if their number included a few members of considerable means, most of them were from the lower classes. Neither their number nor means were enough to build churches. They probably held their rituals in the synagogue (not located), if permitted, or in caves or private houses.

A twenty-metre tunnel dug in the slope of Mt Coressus above the Temple of Serapis is thought to be an early Christian shrine. It contains niches for lamps and offerings and religious graffiti. This situation continued until Constantine the Great. The Edict of Milan (313) restored the property that Christians had lost by persecution edicts and provided the church with the material support of the state.

The building of the earliest churches in Ephesus must have begun during this period. However, because of the permanent political struggle of the previous century there was a shortage of craftsmen in the empire and whatever they built seems to have fallen into ruins shortly after. The building projects begun by Constantine the Great in the capital might have drained the provinces of good architects and builders.

A church probably dedicated to St John, rose on the ruins of the Temple of Serapis in the great agora but there is as yet no information about its date. A large first-century Roman monument to the east of the upper agora, dedicated to heroes, was turned into another church. It is known as the Tomb of St Luke; the name being inspired by the ox relief which is carved under a cross here, the animal bringing to mind the tribute of the Evangelist Luke. Chapels were added to the governor's palace and the villa above the theatre. The westernmost tower of the walls of Lysimachus is also known as the 'Prison of St Paul'.

In the fourth or fifth centuries the site of today's Tusan Motel was occupied by a large church whose floor was paved with mosaic. The situation changed in the sixth century. The piety and ambition of Justinian the Great (527-65) seem to have supplied Ephesus with the architects and finance it needed to build better churches than the previous age. The House of the Virgin, the Church of the Virgin (Double Church), the Grotto of the Seven Sleepers in Ephesus and the Church of St John the Theologian in Selçuk are the most important surviving Christian monuments.

The House of the Virgin

Christian tradition about the last part of the Virgin's life after the Crucifixion is divided. According to one version, she remained in Jerusalem, lived with St John and died here.[1] Another tradition holds that St John took the Virgin, who was entrusted to him by Christ on the cross, to Ephesus where she lived for more than a decade before dying there at the age of sixty-four.

During her stay in Ephesus she is said to have often visited the Holy Land and on one of her visits to Jerusalem she became sick and a tomb was built there for her. However, she recovered and returned to Ephesus. The tradition which claims that she died in Jerusalem is said to have derived from this event.

The origin of claims that were made to repudiate the tradition that the Virgin spent the last part of her life in Ephesus go back to the fourth century, and consequently show that the traditions that they were intended to repudiate were older. Also, the fact that the Third Ecumenical Council was held in Ephesus in the first church dedicated to the Virgin, which accepted the presence of the Virgin in Ephesus, show the strength of this tradition.

The House of the Virgin stands on the mountain known as Solmissus (Aladağ) some seven kilometres from the ruins of Ephesus. The history of the building is thought to date from the fourth century. However, no archaeological investigation has been made as to whether the foundations go back to the first century.

The place was identified by the Lazarists of Smyrna in 1891 on the basis of a German nun named Anne

[1] This tradition holds that St John was martyred in 44 and the Virgin died on Mt Zion in Jerusalem where now the Church of the Dormition exists.

Plan of the House of the Virgin. It is thought that the site which originally served as a House for the Virgin was overbuilt in the sixth century as a chapel of cross-form and later more rooms were added to it.

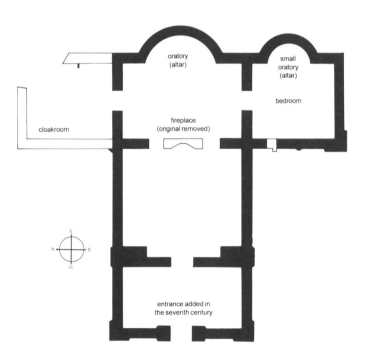

oratory
(altar)

small
oratory
(altar)

bedroom

fireplace
(original removed)

cloakroom

entrance added in
the seventh century

Statue of the Virgin at the entrance of the House of the Virgin near Ephesus.

Catherine Emmerich (1774-1824) who claimed to have seen it in her dream in the early nineteenth century. Even before its rediscovery the local Christians following the tradition of their forefathers, used to gather every year at this small chapel to celebrate the Death of the Virgin whom they called *Panaya Kapulu* a Greek-Turkish name which means 'Gate' or 'House of Our Lady'.

Catherine Emmerich who received the stigmata of the Lord was bedridden and had never been out of Westphalia in Germany. She claimed that 'Mary did not live in Ephesus itself, but in the country near it where several women who were her close friends had settled. Mary's dwelling was on a hill to the left of the road from Jerusalem some three and a half hours from Ephesus. This hill slopes steeply towards Ephesus; the city as one approaches it from the south-east seems to lie on rising ground immediately before one, but seems to change its place as one draws nearer.

Mary's house was the only one built of stone. A little way behind it was the summit of the rocky hill from which one could see over the trees and hills to Ephesus and the sea with its many islands. The place is nearer the sea than Ephesus, which must be several hours' journey distant from the coast. Between the Blessed Virgin's dwelling and Ephesus runs a little stream which winds about in a very singular way.'

Since its discovery, the House of the Virgin has been attributed with a variety of cures for hopeless patients by the use of ashes from its fireplace and water coming out of the spring beneath her room. At the time these lines were being written the fireplace had been removed but the spring was still pouring forth its sweet water with healing powers.

The Church of the Virgin (Double Church)

The original building is thought to have been a long and narrow civic basilica built very close to the harbour, probably during the reign of Hadrian (117-38). It rose on the south stoa of a monument dedicated to the Olympian muses. It had apsed rooms at both ends and a row of small rooms which probably served as shops on both sides. The basilica was destroyed by fire at the time of the Goth attack in 262, together with the rest of the buildings near the harbour and lay in ruins for perhaps a century. Almost nothing survives from this basilica because its ruins became the major source of building material for a number of structures on the same ground.

The first church was probably built in the middle of the fourth century. This was a smaller building than the original basilica. It consisted of a large courtyard, a narthex and a nave with aisles and an apse. Its floor was decorated with mosaics and walls covered with marble revetments. An octagonal baptistry with a large and deep basin which was reached by stairs for total immersion was added to the north of its courtyard. At the eastern end enough space to build a bishop's palace and office rooms was left. The ruins of the complex consist of a large house with a colonnaded courtyard and a bath of several rooms with a latrine.

The fact that the church is known as the first of its kind dedicated to the Virgin is regarded as an evidence that there was a very early tradition which accepted that her last years were spent at Ephesus. Excavations have revealed a sixth-century inscription indicating that the church

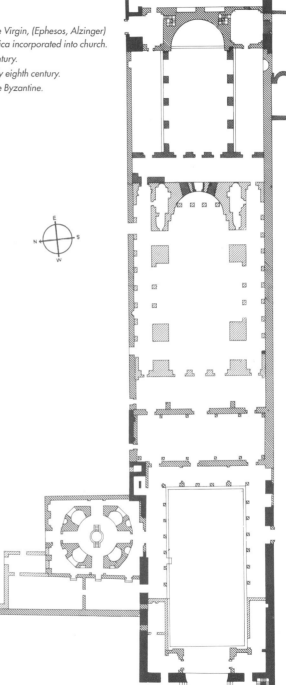

(opposite) Church of the Virgin in Ephesus (looking east).

Baptistry of the church of the Virgin in Ephesus. Early Byzantine period.

church was the site of the Third Ecumenical Council summoned in Ephesus in 431.

Here it was confirmed that the Virgin is the mother of Christ's human and divine natures, because the two can not be divided; this condemned the teaching of Nestorius, bishop of Constantinople, who held that the Virgin could only be the mother of the human aspect of Christ. Thus, it was reconfirmed that the Virgin was *Theotokos*, the Mother of God not *Chrestotokos*, the Mother of Christ. The council also accepted that the Virgin lived in Ephesus with St John.

In the seventh or early eighth century, at the time of the Sassanian and Arab invasions, both the church and the baptistry were destroyed and a smaller domed church of brick was built, probably in the early eighth century. This domed building occupied the western part of the ground of the ancient basilica.

By the Middle Byzantine period this church had fallen into disrepair and another church was built into the space between the apse of the original church and the second one causing the site to be known as the Double Church. The entrance to the latter was through the apse of the second church. Its roof was carried by piers instead of columns. The nave of the second church became its atrium and its diaconicon,[1] a baptistry. The new room added to the south side was probably a burial chapel.

During the later part of its history this last church was rebuilt with two rows of columns to support its roof, turning it into a five-aisled building. By the end of the thirteenth century the area was turned into a cemetery.

[1] The sacristy to the south of the bema; opposite the prothesis.

The Church of St John the Theologian

According to one Christian tradition, during the last part of his life St John withdrew from Ephesus to the hill of Ayasuluk[1] near the Temple of Artemis; building a small hut, he lived here. The hill had no fresh water and was uninhabited until late antiquity. The story claims that he wrote the Fourth Gospel and died at the age of hundred and twenty and was buried here. When he was told by Christ that his end was near, he dug his grave in the form of a cross and lay down in it. The disciples who stood by were blinded by a great light and when their sight was restored they were astonished to find St John's body no longer there, and that a sweet odour arose from manna in the tomb.

Another tradition holds that he slept here in his tomb waiting for the Second Coming, and showed signs of life by scattering the dust, called manna, which healed the sick.

The oldest of the stories attributing the existence of St John's tomb here, date to the second century at which time the hill served as a Roman cemetery. The fragments of a second century sarcophagus found here reputedly belonged to St John. The hill continued to be used as a necropolis during the later Christian period.

The first monument erected on the tomb was probably a small square martyrium.

In the fourth century this was replaced by a three-aisled cruciform church with arms radiating from the tomb. Its

[1] A tradition has it that after he ascended to heaven the earth on the grave of St John kept moving as if stirred by his breathing. The word derives from the Greek *Agios Theologos* thought to mean 'Holy Breath' or 'Aya Soluk' in Turkish, inspired by the signs of life it showed.

Dedicatory cross on steps from one of the columns flanking the entrance of the southern aisle of Church of St John the Theologian. Byzantine period. Selçuk.

47

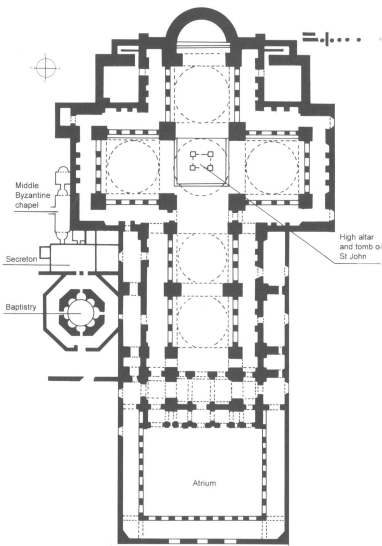

Middle Byzantine chapel

Secreton

Baptistry

High altar and tomb of St John

Atrium

architecture imitated that of the Church of the Holy Apostles built by Constantine the Great in Constantinople. It is also claimed that the shape of the building was inspired by the tradition that St John dug his own grave in the form of a cross and lay down in it.

By the sixth century the building was in disrepair and a new and larger church was erected by Justinian the Great. This church was the largest project undertaken in Anatolia outside the capital. Its plan followed that of the previous church in its general lines but it was larger and more elaborate. It was entered from a courtyard surrounded by a colonnaded portico built partly on the terrace partly obtained by vaulting over the sloping hill. Access to the nave was by a long and narrow narthex topped by five small domes. The plan of the actual building was in the

Plan of the Church of St John the Theologian (*Alzinger*)

Icon of St John the Theologian from the Monastery of St Barnabas in North Cyprus. Nineteenth century. The inscription in Greek, reads *In the beginning was the Word, and the Word was with God, and the Word was God. He was in the beginning with God. All things came to be through him, and without him nothing came to be. What came to be through him was life, and this life was the light of the human race; the light shines in the darkness, and the darkness has not overcome it (Jn 1:1-5).*

form of a cross. Its nave consisted of four bays covered with domes which rested on marble columns and brick buttresses faced with marble. The building probably had galleries. The capitals of the columns bore the monograms of Justinian and Theodora. Under the third dome was the Tomb of St John, reached by a flight of steps; over the tomb was the altar.

Most of the building material came from the ruins of the basilica which stood in the upper agora of Ephesus (destroyed probably by an earthquake around 500) and from the ruins of the Temple of Artemis just below the hill. The floor was covered with geometric mosaics, the walls and domes had mosaics and frescoes depicting subjects from the Old and New Testaments.

On the north side was a large octagonal baptistry with stairs for total immersion, bringing to mind that of the Double Church. The rectangular room next to it was the 'secreton' where the bishop presided as judge. An aqueduct was built to supply fresh water from the spring in the eastern heights some ten kilometres away.

During the Arab raids in the seventh and eighth centuries the hill was surrounded by a wall and became a part of the castle built on the summit. It was probably during this insecure period that the people of the town began to settle on the hill. Nevertheless, the hill and its monuments were sacked during the invasions. The buildings which stood on the hilltop were restored afterwards. The exonarthex is thought to have been added during this period.

In the tenth century a chapel decorated with frescoes was built to the north of the church.

In the fourteenth century, until the construction of İsa Bey Mosque, the former church served as the principal mosque of the city.

The remains of the apsed structure at the top of the hill date from the sixth century and were used as a cistern during the Turkish period. The ruin is claimed to be the oratory of St John where he wrote the Fourth Gospel. Tradition has it that the event was initiated by Sts Peter and Paul who visited St John here and pursuaded him to write his Gospel, which it is said that he did in an hour.

Neither ancient tradition nor modern research agree whether the Fourth Gospel and the book of Revelation and the Letters attributed to St John were written by the same or different people and whether St John the Theologian, or the 'Divine' or St John the Apostle and St John the Evangelist are the same or different persons. However, popular Christian tradition accepted that the church which stood here was erected on the Tomb of St John the Theologian who is known as the Evangelist and the Apostle.

On July 26, 1967, Pope Paul VI offered supplication here.

Marble revetment of Byzantine period from the church of St John the Theologian. Selçuk.

51

The Grotto of
the Seven Sleepers

According to Christian tradition of late antiquity a young Christian boy appeared in Ephesus one day in the mid-fifth century to buy food with coins two hundred years old. When accused of forgery and brought to court, the young man, who was named Maxianus, claimed that he and his friends (Malchus, Martianus, Constantine, Dionysius, John and Serapion) had refused cult rituals for the emperor Decius (249-51); taking shelter in a cave at the foot of Mt Pion they had gone to sleep. It seemed that they had slept for two hundred years.

This happened at the time of the outbreak of the controversy about the resurrection of the Christ's body and their story was welcomed by the local church and was regarded true.

When they died, the boys were buried in the cave in which they had fallen asleep and a church was built over it by Theodosius II (408-50).[1] In the course of time the cave and vicinity became a sought-after burial ground and graves of various sorts filled the area. Excavations have brought to light a large number of lamps decorated with Old Testament subjects and popular scenes from the pagan repertory. The cave became a popular spot of pilgrimage and as the graffiti show, it was visited by believers throughout the Byzantine period until the end of the fifteenth century.

The northern section of the complex seems to have been carved out of an ancient quarry. It consists of a long vaulted crypt which begins with two smaller rooms. It has burial niches in the walls and under the floor. It is decorated with frescoes of garlands and baskets.

The large complex near this consists of a long vaulted room and catacombs below its floor. The latter are thought to have contained the Tombs of the Seven Sleepers. Nothing survives from the church which originally stood opposite.

The site must have undergone more than a single stage of decoration. A mosaic of saints in the vestibule of the crypt was added in the eighth or ninth century. Two layers of frescoes of saints and crosses in the catacomb were painted in the tenth and eleventh centuries. The frescoes at the entrance of the catacombs are probably from the Lascarid period (1204-61).

The excavation has shown that the use of the north slope of Mt Pion as a cemetery goes beyond the Christian era. In addition to the Seven Sleepers, St Timothy, St Hermione and Mary Magdalene, who is said to have joined St John in Ephesus after the death of the Virgin, are said to have been buried on or near Mt Pion.

[1] Mosaics and frescoes of the church have given scholars the impression that it was probably built at the time of Theodosius I (379-95).

ANCIENT SMYRNA

The earliest settlement of Smyrna (Tepekule tumulus at Bayraklı) was on a small peninsula along the Aegean, probably as early as the first half of the third millennium BCE. At the beginning of the first millennium the migrations of the Dark Ages seem to have brought Greeks here.

Thereafter, the city developed and like Ephesus or Miletus became one of the most wealthy *poleis* of the region. The most important building of this period was the Temple of Athena whose origins went back to the end of the seventh century BCE. In 600 BCE the city was captured by the Lydians and later in 545 BCE by the Persians. However, it never recovered its ancient glory and by 300 BCE people began moving to the outskirts of Mt Pagus (Kadifekale).

A later tradition attributes the foundation of the city at its new location to Alexander the Great. Whilst dreaming on Mt Pagus, he was asked by the Nemeseis, the goddesses of the mountain, to found a city here. Even if only the foundation stone had been laid by him and the actual building was done by Lysimachus, Alexander is regarded as the traditional founder of Smyrna.

The city with its deep sheltered harbour prospered, and became along with Ephesus the most important coastal city of Asia Minor. The stadium and theatre were situated on the slope of Mt Pagus which had become the acropolis of the Hellenistic city. The rest of the monuments, such as the Temples of Homer, Cybele or the Nemeseis were on the plain. Most of these continued in use under Roman rule.

In 195 BCE Rome allowed Smyrna to erect a temple of the goddess Roma for her help in Rome's struggle against the Seleucids. There is nothing left from the Hellenistic city and from the Roman period only the ruins of the agora survive.

At the time that St Polycarp became its bishop the city's population was close to a hundred thousand people. Marble crosses found in the Agora indicate the existence of a sixth century church. St John's letter in the Revelation shows that there was a synagogue in the city during the first century.

The modern city is built on the ancient site so little excavation is possible. In 654 and 672 it was captured by Arabs. However, during the Lascarid rule (1204-61) it was still one of the largest cities and the major harbour of the area. Research has shown that the date of some fragments of the Byzantine masonry on Mt Pagus go back to the Roman and Hellenistic periods.

To the church in Smyrna

To the angel of the church in Smyrna, write this:

'The first and the last, who once died but came to life, says this: "I know your tribulation and poverty, but you are rich. I know the slander of those who claim to be Jews and are not, but rather are members of the assembly of Satan. Do not be afraid of anything that you are going to suffer. Indeed, the devil will throw some of you into prison, that you may be tested, and you will face an ordeal for ten days. Remain faithful until death, and I will give you the crown of life.'

Whoever has ears ought to hear what the Spirit says to the churches. The victor shall not be harmed by the second death.

(Rv 2:8-11).

In his letter to the church in Smyrna St John introduces Christ as the first and the last, an expression repeated at the end of the Revelation as *I am Alpha and Omega,*[1] *the first and the last, the beginning and the end* (Rv 21:6), and as the living one who has passed through death and come to life. The same imagery is found at the beginning of his letters (Rv 1:18) as *I am the Alpha and the*

Omega, *the one who is and who was and who is to come, the almighty*. It is inspired by the Greek concept of using the alphabet as a symbol of cosmological totality, here, referring to the totality of the Divine world of Christian faith.

He informs the Christians that he is familiar with both the suffering and poverty of their community, a material poverty probably caused by Roman oppression and that of the synagogue Jews who did not accept Christianity. The hatred of such Jews for Christians was known to extend to physical violence. The city was renowned for its loyalty to Rome and for the hatred of its Jews for Christians.

The expression *the assembly of Satan* is also encountered in his letter to the church in Philadelphia. Like other Christian writers St John uses the word 'assembly' (Greek *synagogue*) to refer to the Jewish community or to the building in which they met. He sees the word as the 'symbol of the Jewish religion of law and tradition.' This may be the reason Christian authors tried to avoid its use, preferring instead Greek *ekklesia*, which also meant 'assembly' or 'church'.

In his gospel St John sees the Jews as a *symbol of human evil* and as ally of Satan. Christians are known to have distinguished themselves not only from Jews but from pagans as well. Gentile Christians and the Jewish Christians who called themselves 'true Jews' were attacked by the other Jews.

However, the ordeal St John has in mind would last only ten days — a period whose meaning is not clear. It

[1] The first and last letters of the Greek alphabet.

The Forty Martyrs of Sebaste with their crowns waiting for them at the feet of Christ. Icon from Ayasofya Museum, İstanbul. Seventeenth-eighteenth centuries. Tradition has it that forty soldiers of a Roman legion stationed in Sebaste (Sivas) who had accepted Christianity, refused the command of the emperor Licinius to abandon their faith in 320. They were forced to spend the night on a frozen lake. At the centre the martyrs are shown naked partly submerged in the lake of ice. Those who had not died by the next morning were killed and their remains burned. On the right, with smoke coming out, is a hot bath intended as an extra inducement of apostasy, a soldier stands in front. One of the figures has stepped forward towards the bath thus abandoning his faith. At the top Christ standing half-length in heaven and the forty crowns of martyrdom (with one cancellation) descending in glory are represented.

Relief with a gladiator in Ephesus. The figure wears armour together with helmet, shield, sword and greaves. Before him is a victor's palm. Roman period.

is claimed that *ten days* may refer to a limited period of tribulation. In the book of Daniel 1:12 where the hero says to the official of the Babylonian king Nebuchadnezzar: *Please test your servants for ten days*, it means just a certain period of time. On the other hand this may have been related to a specific tradition. An inscription on the base of a statue of a high priest of the imperial cult discovered in the agora mentions that he arranged gladiator shows for five days. Similar inscriptions from Thyateira, Pergamum and other cities of the Roman world show that during this period the mentioning of the duration of such spectacles was not unusual. St John may have had in mind such a meaning when he used the words *an ordeal of ten days*. The story of martyrdoms shows that the persecutions of Christians during such spectacles — before the gladiatorial games began — was not uncommon.

According to St John their persecution for the faith has brought them spiritual richness. If they stick to their faith their reward will be the *crown of life*. This imagery commonly brings to mind Christ's crown of thorns, the symbol of martyrdom and suffering but essentially a crown of life 'everlasting'. The metaphor may have been inspired by the fact that the crown or wreath was the most common element on the coins issued in Smyrna and the prize of Christian martyrs. They are probably imagined as athletes winning their 'crowns' in the stadium. St John ends his letter by referring to his words in the book of Revelation (Rv 20:14) that the *victor*, who has been martyred will not be hurt by *the pool of fire* that is the second death.

St Polycarp

Modern scholars generally think that the Christian martyrdom stories are highly exaggerated and that if Roman persecution had been as severe as claimed, Christianity would have been an underground movement never able to reach large groups. Also, early Christian leaders, in order to encourage their flocks who may have lost hope and courage, are thought to have chosen this sort of self-sacrifice, following the path of Christ and ensuring their popularity both in this world and the one to come. Popular punishments reserved for Christians were crucifixion, burning or being thrown to wild animals, with the latter two often carried out in open places of assembly.

The story of the martyrdom of St Polycarp is regarded as the first authentic narrative of a Christian martyrdom and is a typical example of the persecutions that Christian leaders suffered. His story gives detailed information of how he was arrested and martyred by the mob of Smyrna.

St Polycarp is thought to have lived in about 69-156, and met some of the apostles who had known Christ. He is thought to have been converted by St John and appointed by him to his post as the bishop of Smyrna.

The persecution of Christians in Smyrna was probably no more frequent than in any other Roman city. It was carried out in the stadium[1] near the southern fortifications of the city and close to the sea. During one such spectacle the crowd having been frustrated by the calmness and composure with which the young Christian victim Germanicus met his death, began shouting for St Polycarp to be brought for punishment.

When his friends learned that the Roman authorities were looking for him, St Polycarp was taken outside the city and moved from one farm to the other to mislead his searchers. Nevertheless, finally he was arrested and brought to the stadium. The efforts of the proconsul to pursuade him take oath to the emperor and curse Christ were useless. The story of St Polycarp's martyrdom is narrated in a letter written from the church in Smyrna to the church in Philomelium (Akşehir). According to this St Polycarp answered the authorities as:

> 'For eighty and six years' St Polycarp answered them 'I have been His servant and He has never done me wrong. How can I blaspheme my king, who has saved me.'

St Polycarp was finally sentenced to death by burning, as he had foreseen earlier in his life. At his own request he was not lashed to a stake but his hands were tied behind his back. He met his end with a look of joy on his face. It was claimed that the flames enveloped his form like the sails of a ship swelled with the wind:

> And there was he in the centre of it, not like a human being in flames but like a loaf baking in the oven, or like a gold or silver ingot being refined in the furnace. And we became aware of a delicious fragrance, like the odour of incense or other precious gums.

This is the reason that he was sometimes represented with flames surrounding him like a halo. However, when it was realized that the fire had not destroyed him, he was stabbed. After his death his body was burned to ashes which his disciples collected and buried.

[1] Its site is completely built over and there is no trace of it.

Detail from the reliefs of the Great Altar of Pergamum which is restored and displayed in the Pergamum Museum, Berlin. It shows a Giant being attacked by the dog of Artemis. Mid-second century BCE.

ANCIENT PERGAMUM

Pergamum was, at the time that the new religion travelled along the caravan routes of Asia Minor or was carried by trade ships which brought olive oil from Cilicia or copper from Cyprus to its port Elaea, one of the largest cities of the region. Its wealth, number of temples and their beauty were eclipsed only by those of Ephesus.

By the first century the Hellenistic city on the acropolis was no longer large enough to accommodate the growing population and the city began to spread to the valley extending towards the Asclepion. The history of Pergamum began after the death of Lysimachus, one of Alexander's generals. In 281 BCE when Lysimachus was killed in the battle of Curupedion against the Seleucids, Philetairos, governor of Pergamum, found himself in control of the city and owner of a large treasury which he spent making the city stronger. Under a series of able and energetic rulers, Pergamum became one of the most important powers of the area.

Under Eumenes II (197-159 BCE) the whole of western Asia Minor was acquired from Rome for his help during the battle of Magnesia against the Seleucids (190 BCE) Pergamum became the sole kingdom of the region.

Eumenes II is remembered for the Great Altar that he

Statue of the emperor Hadrian discovered in the library of the Asclepion. Bergama Archaeological Museum.

(opposite) Ruins of the Temple of Trajan on the acropolis of Pergamum (looking towards Bergama).

built on the acropolis. This is one of the most important monuments of the Hellenistic period.

Attalos III who did not have a legitimate heir, probably realized that the end of Pergamum was inevitable and in order to prevent war over the succession, bequeathed his kingdom to Rome on his death in 133 BCE.

The city continued to grow under the patronship of its Roman rulers. Along with Ephesus, it was the earliest city where the Roman imperial cult was established. As the seat of a Hellenistic kingdom, people were familiar with the concept of ruler cult which was practised in the Hellenistic heroön whose ruins have survived.

The arrival of Rome gave new vigour to the city. Skillful builders, they made terraces on vaults and erected new temples, baths and other civic buildings. While the Attalids had used andesite, which was the local mountain stone, new buildings were in marble. The ruins of the asclepion, stadium and amphitheatre are all Roman. After those in Cos and Epidauros, the Asclepion of Pergamum was the most important medical centre in the Roman Empire.

The city's prosperous history continued until the Arab conquests in 663 and 716. Unable to revive thereafter its acropolis was used as a Byzantine stronghold and then fell into oblivion.

To the church in Pergamum

To the angel of the church in Pergamum, write this:

The one with the sharp two-edged sword says this: 'I know that you live where Satan's throne is, and yet you hold fast to my name and have not denied your faith in me, not even in the days of Antipas, my faithful witness, who was martyred among you, where Satan lives. Yet I have a few things against you. You have some people there who hold to the teaching of Balaam, who instructed Balak to put a stumbling block before the Israelites: to eat food sacrificed to idols and to play the harlot. Likewise, you also have some people who hold to the teaching of (the) Nicolaitans. Therefore, repent. Otherwise, I will come to you quickly and wage war against them with the sword of my mouth.'

Whoever has ears ought to hear what the Spirit says to the churches. To the victor I shall give some of the hidden manna; I shall also give a white amulet upon which is inscribed a new name, which no one knows except the one who receives it.

(Rv 2:12-17)

At the beginning of the letter to this church St John introduces Christ as the one who has the two-edged sword. The allusion comes from the letter to the Hebrews

Base of the statue of Augustus at the centre of the court of the Temple of Athena on the acropolis of Pergamum. The marble floor behind it belonged to the Byzantine church which is thought to have been erected during the reign of Justinian the Great.

Marble capital from the Church of St John the Theologian in the Red Court. Pergamum.

(Heb 4:12): *Indeed, the word of God is living and effective, sharper than any two-edged sword, penetrating even between soul and spirit, joints and marrow and able to discern reflections and thoughts of the heart.* Also in the book of Psalms (149:6) Jews are invited to stand with a *two-edged sword* in their hands to defend Zion.

When St John addressed the third of his letters in the Revelation to Pergamum, the city was one of the most important centres of paganism, including the imperial cult of the region. At the time that the letter was written, there was a statue of the divine Augustus in the temenos of Athena's Temple on the summit of the acropolis; there might also have been a statue of the goddess Roma. These were the earliest monuments of the Roman imperial cult in the city.

The Great Altar whose walls were decorated with reliefs showing the battle of Greek gods with the Giants also stood on the acropolis. Some scholars claim that when St John referred to the *Satan's throne* he had the Great Altar in mind. St John was probably concerned with the imperial cult more than the older Hellenistic cults, which had begun to loosen their hold on the people. On the plain stood the famous sanctuary of Asclepius, the temple of the healer-god, which attracted pilgrims and patients from distant corners of the world. Other scholars believe that this referred to the mystical chest (cyst) in which was kept a live serpent, a special object of veneration in the Asclepion, or the sanctuary itself.

St John praises the Christians of Pergamum for not having given up their faith despite all the pressure on them. Antipas, one of the spiritual leaders of the Pergamene congregation, was martyred by being roasted in a brazen bull. In the New Testament the Greek word *martyr* meaning 'witness' or 'testimony'[1] is used for bearing witness to the faith in Christ to the end of one's life and used only twice meaning 'slain': at the stoning of St Stephen and here at the martyrdom of Antipas.

It seems that despite their faith in the new religion, some of the Christians in Pergamum were practicing the heresy of Balaam. The book of Numbers (Nm 22-25 and 31:16) relates that after going out of Egypt, during their wanderings to reach the Promised Land, the Israelites drew the Amorites out of their land and set their camp near the land of the Moabites. The king of the latter, Balak, was afraid that his people would suffer the fate of the Amorites and sent for the Old Testament prophet Balaam to curse the Israelites. However, Balaam was unable to do so. In the end, although it is not told how Balaam induced them, the people of Israel began engaging in prostitution with Moabite women[2] and began to eat food sacrificed to gods by their neighbours (1 Kgs 16:31 and 2 Kgs 9:22, 30-37).

In Pergamum there are also those who believe in the teaching of the Nicolaitans, like their brothers in Ephesus. After having acknowledged the problems in Pergamum,

[1] In the course of time the word would gain its present day meaning.

[2] The worship of the Semitic god Baal required cultic prostitution.

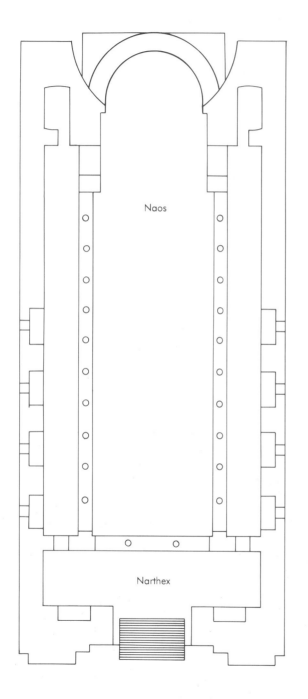

Naos

Narthex

Plan of the Church of St John the Theologian in the Red Court (W. Radt).

(opposite) Ruins of the Red Court with the remains of the Church of St John the Theologian (looking west from the apse).

St John admonishes those who waver to repent and threatens them that Christ will come for them with the sword in his mouth — again referring to the impending Second Coming. The believers who conquer — who have not eaten food sacrificed to idols — will be rewarded. Their reward will be *the hidden manna*, the food that God gave the Israelites as they wandered in the wilderness, in the sense that it will nourish their spirits forever. Each member of the church is also to be given a *white amulet*, with a new name, a name of glory.

Excavations have brought to light the remains of a number of church buildings in ancient Pergamum. The best known of these is the Church of St John that was built into the so-called Red Court. This was probably built in the fourth century and served as the cathedral of the city.

Another church of the early period occupied the courtyard of the lower agora but has no visible remains at present. A third one occupied the site of the enclosure of the Temple of Athena on top of the acropolis. This was built during the time of Justinian the Great and some of its marble floor pavement still survives. The Christians who lived in the Asclepion district had their own churches here. Archaeologists have also distinguished traces of other less important church buildings among the ruins dating from the later Byzantine period.

It is assumed that in Pergamum as elsewhere, the Christian community included some Jewish converts. Although a gable from a synagogue door or screen showing a menorah has been discovered, the place where the synagogue was located is not known.

ANCIENT THYATEIRA

The oldest information about Thyateira (Akhisar) is that as early as the seventh century BCE a Lydian castle stood here. The Seleucid king Antiochus I is known to have founded a number of military establishments controlling the possible invasion routes from central Anatolia, which was ruled by the Galatians. Thyateira must have been one of these strongholds but there is no information as to how large the settlement became. However, it continued serving as a stronghold for Hellenistic Pergamum and later, also under the Romans.

Before facing the latter at the battle of Magnesia in 190 BCE, the Seleucid forces camped here. During the battle the Roman forces were commanded by Lucius Cornelius Scipio with his famous brother Scipio Africanus as his aide. Among the allies of Rome, it was Eumenes II of Pergamum who distinguished himself in the battle. The struggle ended with the victory of Rome and as a reward Eumenes II gained the possession of the area north of Ephesus. Since Thyateira stood in the path of any invader who would approach Pergamum, from the south, the Pergamene rulers kept a military garrison in the town. In 133 BCE when the last king of Pergamum Attalos III, left his kingdom to Rome the city became Roman property.

Like the rest of western Anatolia, Thyateira suffered the invasions of the Goths in the middle of the third century and of Arabs in the seventh and eighth centuries. It later became a Byzantine stronghold against the Turkish Emirates and saw some flourishing days under the Lascarids.

The limited excavations which could be done at the centre of the present day city have brought to light the ruins of two important structures.

The first group belongs to an apsed construction which is thought to date from the fifth or sixth century. Its walls which were of rubble with lime mortar and reinforced with layers of brick survive to a height of some four and half metres. Its southern part must have been destroyed during the construction of the modern street. To the west the building was flanked by some rectangular halls. Since no artefact remains which indicates the presence of a church this building is thought to be a civil basilica with various functions.

The second group of ruins belongs to a portico (monumental entrance) which stood to the west of a colonnaded street. The marble colonnade of the portico stood to the height of some five metres. Plinths, stylobates, columns and capitals visible today are thought to date from the second century. The arches which joined the columns are from the fourth century. Its roof was probably wood. Two doors gave access to the premises at the back.

The eastern side of the colonnaded street still lies under the modern street and its width cannot be calculated. It had a rubble path sloping towards the edges.

Among all the cities to which St John's letters are addressed, Thyateira was the only one which was founded on flat land without natural defences. Thus it was invaded and plundered easily by the armies which passed through the area, often by those on their way to Pergamum. Like most other cities Thyateira must have had a Jewish colony and a Christian community would have developed by the second half of the first century.

According to the Acts of the Apostles the first Christian that St Paul encountered on European soil was a native of Thyateira. This happened during the second journey of St Paul in the middle of the first century. St Paul left Antioch with Silas. They travelled by way of Cilicia, Phrygia and Galatia. In Lystra, Timothy joined them. When they reached the border of Mysia and Bithynia on which Thyateira was located the Spirit of Christ stopped them. Paul and his friends turned to the direction of Troas and

took a ship to Samothrace and then to Neapolis. From here they went to Philippi.

Philippi was named after Philip of Macedon, father of Alexander the Great, and at the time that Paul and his friends preached it was a thriving Roman colony on the *via Egnatia*, the main road to Rome. Lydia, the woman they met here, was a dealer in purple which together with the production of other colours — especially the red of madder root — must have been one of the sources of the wealth of Thyateira. The coins of Thyateira display the existence of guilds of bakers, bronzesmiths, wool workers, potters, linen weavers and tanners; probably the richest collection of guilds among the cities of Asia Minor during this period, and these probably had trade representatives at Philippi.

The Acts of the Apostles (Acts 16:11-16) reads:

> *We set sail from Troas, making a straight run for Samothrace, and on the next day to Neapolis, and from there to Philippi, a leading city in that district of Macedonia and a Roman colony. We spent some time in that city. On the sabbath we went outside the city gate along the river where we thought there would be a place of prayer. We sat and spoke with the women who had gathered there. One of them, a woman named Lydia, a dealer in purple cloth, from the city of Thyateira, a worshiper of God, listened, and the Lord opened her heart to pay attention to what Paul was saying. After she and her household had been baptized, she offered us an invitation, 'If you consider me a believer in the Lord, come and stay at my home,' and she prevailed on us.*

Marble cross decorated with leaves from Thyateira. Byzantine period. Manisa Archaeological Museum.

To the church in Thyateira

To the angel of the church in Thyateira, write this:

'The Son of God, whose eyes are like a fiery flame and whose feet are like polished brass, says this: "I know your works, your love, faith, service, and endurance, and that your last works are greater than the first. Yet I hold this against you, that you tolerate the woman Jezebel, who calls herself a prophetess, who teaches and misleads my servants to play the harlot and to eat food sacrificed to idols. I have given her time to repent, but she refuses to repent of her harlotry. So I will cast her on a sickbed and plunge those who commit adultery with her into intense suffering unless they repent of her works. I will also put her children to death. Thus shall all the churches come to know that I am the searcher of hearts and minds and that I will give each of you what your works deserve. But I say to the rest of you in Thyateira, who do not uphold this teaching and know nothing of the so-called deep secrets of Satan: on you I will place no further burden, except that you must hold fast to what you have until I come.

"To the victor, who keeps to my ways until the end, I will give authority over the nations.

He will rule them with an iron rod. Like clay vessels will they be smashed,

Just as I received authority from my Father. And to him I will give the morning star.

"Whoever has ears ought to hear what the Spirit says to the churches." '
(Rv 2:18-29)

St John's letter to the church in Thyateira which was materially the most insignificant of the seven cities in fact is the longest. This is not a coincidence but probably an imperative caused by the gravity of the situation in the church in Thyateira. The city was known for the popularity of its pagan trade-guilds and the church here must have felt their strong pressure.

At the beginning of the letter St John uses the imagery he has already employed in the introduction of the book of Revelation. As in the book of Daniel, God is described like a pagan deity, with eyes like a flame of fire which could penetrate into everything and feet like polished brass which could walk on anything. The imagery is appropriate as Thyateira was known for its bronzesmiths. He praises the church for enduring the stages of persecutions patiently. He may have in mind those which are said to have taken place either under Gaius (Caligula) and Nero, or Nero and Domitian.

The Christians of Thyateira, however, have another major problem. This is their toleration of the activities of a woman called Jezebel who claimed that she was a prophetess — probably a priestess of the Sibylline[1] oracle in the city. It is known that such oracles were very popular during the period and their prophecy was asked for not only by pagans but by Jews and Christians. St John calling this woman Jezebel alludes to the daughter of the Phoenician king of Sidon who married the king Ahab of Israel and he describes her teaching as that of Balaam (1 Kgs 16:31 and 2 Kgs 9:22, 30-37), eating things sacrificed to idols and committing sexual immorality. This woman, for whom St John has used the nickname Jezebel, seems to have been able to lead many Christians in Thyateira to worship pagan gods like her Old Testament namesake.[2] The Lord gave her a chance to repent. But it was useless, she continued her evil ways. For this both the woman and those who are tempted by her teaching will be punished. The punishment will also cover her children, that is those who will follow her teaching even after her death. God sees, tests and searches the hidden depths of the human heart.

There are however, those who hold fast against such evil temptations, those who have not known the *deep secrets of Satan* and those who have not participated in the ungodly things of this world, probably the teaching of Nicolaitans. St John advises these to wait a little longer until Christ comes when they will receive power over nations and the morning star. The metaphors are derived from Psalms 2:9:

> *You shall rule them with an iron rod;*
> *you shall shatter them like an earthen*
> *dish*

the metal being the symbol of endurance and hardness, from the images of victorious Christ in the book of Revelation where he is referred to as ruling the conquered nations. The *morning star* or 'Venus' is the symbol of daybreak, and so of sovereignty and victory over death.

The traces of the Christian history of Thyateira do not amount to much. Although its date is not known, Ulu Cami or the Grand Mosque is regarded as the oldest in the city. The large stone blocks visible in its southwestern corner, its southern wall and an arcade on this side go back to the pre-Christian period when it probably served first as a pagan temple and afterwards a civil basilica. Its church history is indicated by the curved trace of half of an apse outside the eastern wall. Some of the columns in the building are also thought to be re-used church material.

The few column pieces which still lie in the courtyard of Şeyhisa Cami, the Sheikh Jesus Mosque, may indicate the existence of another church here.

The other remains related to Christianity from Thyateira are displayed in Manisa Archaeological Museum.

[1] A name thought to refer to female seers of Apollo who prophesied in an ecstatic state.

[2] After marrying her in accordance with the custom of the time Ahab had a temple of Baal built for his queen.

ANCIENT SARDIS

Sardis (Sartmustafa) is thought to have been founded at the end of the second millennium BCE. During this period it was probably the capital of one of the local principalities which stood along the western border of the Hittites. The rock reliefs near İzmir and Manisa show that the power of the Hittites reached this far. From around 1200 BCE and until the beginning of the seventh century BCE little is known about the history of Sardis.

With Gyges[1] (about 685-645 BCE), the first of the Mermnad dynasty, a history albeit sketchy can be traced. It was now that the Cimmerian hordes, who had already destroyed Phrygian Gordion, arrived. Lydia, however, on account of its material resources and efficient rulers recovered quickly. Under the fabled Croesus (561-546 BCE), the last king of the dynasty, Sardis was captured by the Persians.

Ancient sources mention the gifts of gold and silver that the rulers of Lydia sent to the Temples of Apollo at Delphi and Miletus and Artemis of Ephesus. The 'Lud', or Lydians are referred to several times in the Old Testament (Gn 10:22, 1 Chr 1:17 and Is 66:19). In the book of Jeremiah (46:4) 'Men of Lud' (probably mercenaries) in the army of the Pharoah Neco 'stretch' their 'bows' against Nebuchadnezzar, king of Babylon in a battle at Carchemish on the Euphrates in the sixth century BCE.

The richness of the Lydian kingdom came from gold — a natural electrum with a high silver content — washed by rain from Mt Tmolus (Bozdağ) into the Pactolus river (Sartderesi). Research has shown that some of the conglomerate layers of this mountain contain two gr of gold

[1] The name is encountered on the walls of the largest tumuli of Bin Tepe, or One Thousand Mounds, which was the cemetery of Lydian kings and nobles not far away from Sardis. The Assyrian archives of the period refer to this king as 'Gugu' of the Luddi (Lydians).

Hittite relief near Sardis. Fifteenth century BCE. It is thought to represent a Hittite god or the Hittite king Tudhaliyas II (1460-1440 BCE) who is known to have carried out an 'Assuwa' campaign.

per m³. When God is reported as saying in the book of Isaiah 45:3 that he will give Cyrus:

> *treasures out of the darkness, and riches that have been hidden away*

it is thought that the *treasures* may be those Cyrus seized in Sardis. By the time the region was incorporated into the Roman empire, towards the end of the second century BCE, the river's gold content was exhausted.

Until the Lydians invented coinage, gold or silver bars or rings were the popular medium of business transactions. Neither the weight nor the purity of this commodity was guaranteed and the seller had to depend on his own skill not to lose money. The earliest coins manufactured in Lydia were electrum ingots. They bore the stamp of the king guaranteeing their value. Thus, the responsibility moved from the businessman to the ruler. It seems that since the gold content in electrum changed from about 36 to 53 per cent, it became necessary to introduce coins of pure gold. To obtain this high purity the little electrum ingots were hammered into thin sheets and put in a pot in layers with a mixture of brick dust and salt. When the mixture was heated for a long time the salt combined with the silver and left the gold pure. It is said that during this period the amount of gold obtained from the Pactolus river was so great that its value fell to one thirteenth of silver. The invention of coinage was soon copied by the Persians and Greeks.

In the middle of the sixth century BCE the greed of Croesus for the lands beyond the Halys river (Kızılırmak),

Lydian goldworking installations in Sardis.

brought him against Persia. The battle fought in 546 BCE near the Halys river between the forces of Croesus and the Persian king Cyrus the Great ended with the victory of the latter. Cyrus then invaded western Asia Minor, and conquering Sardis made it the capital of the province established here. The city became the centre of the Persian administration in the west. During the Persian rule the Royal Road became the most important artery between the West and the East.[2]

In the autumn of 481 BCE Xerxes I arrived at Sardis with a large army to spend the winter here before setting out for the Hellespont to conquer Greece in the spring. In 401 BCE the younger Cyrus assembled his forces in Sardis before starting his long expedition to Persia to claim the throne from his elder brother Artaxerxes II Mnemon (404-359 BCE).

Persian rule lasted until the arrival of Alexander the Great in 334 BCE. After his death and until 190 BCE, the region was ruled first by Lysimachus and afterwards by the Seleucids. When the latter were defeated by Rome at the battle of Magnesia, the city and the lands belonging to it were given to Eumenes II of Pergamum for the valour he had shown during the battle. When Attalos III left his kingdom to Rome in 133 BCE, Sardis was incorporated into the new Roman province.

The city suffered the earthquakes of 17 and 26 and had to be rebuilt several times. By the end of the first century its population had reached some hundred thousand inhabitants. What has survived to the present day shows that during Roman rule it was one of the most prosperous cities of the region. This prosperity lasted until the Sassanian conquest of 616. After this it became an eastern Roman frontier stronghold and gradually fell into obscurity.

[2] A section of it still waits to be excavated about two metres below the Roman road next to the gymnasium of Sardis.

To the church in Sardis

To the angel of the church in Sardis, write this:

The one who has the seven spirits of God and the seven stars says this: 'I know your works, that you have the reputation of being alive, but you are dead. Be watchful and strengthen what is left, which is going to die, for I have not found your works complete in the sight of my God. Remember then how you accepted and heard; keep it, and repent. If you are not watchful, I will come like a thief, and you will never know at what hour I will come upon you. However, you have a few people in Sardis who have not soiled their garments; they will walk with me dressed in white, because they are worthy.

The victor will thus be dressed in white, and I will never erase his name from the book of life but will acknowledge his name in the presence of my Father and of his angels.'

Whoever has ears ought to hear what the Spirit says to the churches.

(Rv 3:1-6)

The message of St John to the church in Sardis begins with the introduction of Christ as the one who possesses the seven spirits of God and the seven stars. The Spirit of God is symbolized as the seven spirits. The seven stars are the angels of the Seven Churches.

The abrubt manner in which St John begins admonishing

Marble font of reused material from the Byzantine shops situated next to the synagogue in Sardis. The shop is thought to have served ultimately as a baptistry. The crosses were superimposed over pagan inscriptions and decorations.

the church in Sardis, contrasting their present state with the past, gives the impression that it has completely surrendered to the temptations against which St John tries to warn the Christians of the time. These were apostasy or following the teaching of false prophets, worshipping the imperial cult or not embracing the faith heartfully. For this reason the church of Sardis is regarded as *dead*. It exists only in name or materially. It is time that it wakes up from this dead state. Otherwise it will be punished without knowing when this will happen; the latter bringing to mind the impregnable citadel of Sardis which was captured by surprise by Cyrus the Great or Antiochus III. This may be at night as the people of city are asleep, ignorant of the hour of arrival of the punishment.

Nevertheless, there are those few Christians in Sardis who have kept their faith. They are the conquerors. They have not defiled their garments; they have not fallen into heresy. They are worthy of being rewarded with *white garments*, the symbol of eternal bliss, and their names will be confessed before God and his angels. Their names will not be erased from the book of life like those who did not endure the persecutions. The latter derives from Luke 10:20 where Christ tells the seventy-two men to rejoice because their names are written in heaven. It means they belong to God and God's kingdom. The metaphor is found in the book of Daniel (Dn 12:1) where the people whose names *found written in the book* escape distress. In the book of Exodus (32:33) God answers Moses: *only who has sinned against me will I strike out of my book*. Philippians 4:3 also refers to *the book of life*. In the book of Revelation St John says that after the resurrection of the dead, the Last Judgement will take place and the people whose names are not found in the book will be cast into the lake of fire (Rv 20:15). The others (Rv 21:7) will be rewarded with eternal life on a new earth.

A. Northeast enclosure
B. Northwest enclosure
C. East Apse
D. West Apse
1. Fin wall
2-4. Southeast Artemis
    Temple column bases
5. Niche
6. New retaining wall
7. Old drain
8. New drains
9. Destroyed foundation
10. Probable doorstep

Christian Ruins in Sardis

Research has brought to light the ruins of several churches in Sardis. One of these — named 'M' by archaeologists — is situated next to the southeastern corner of the Temple of Artemis and was built to consecrate the pagan Temple and serve as a funerary chapel for a cemetery. Access to it was through the southern colonnade of the temple. The church building consisted of a simple apsidal hall with a window in the apse. It also had clerestory windows which were later filled. A small door in its north wall led to a courtyard. The building had a marble floor of reused material. Its walls were of rubble alternating with brick courses. They were originally plastered over and decorated on the inner and outer sides. The altar consisted of a block of sandstone on a marble support and is one of the earliest altars discovered. The coins found just outside the courtyard door assured archaeologists that the church was built before 400. The larger outer apse with a triforium of the building was added in the sixth century. This part had a door leading to a service room on the north side and another door on the opposite side opened towards the cemetery.

Two churches to the right of the path leading to the Temple of Artemis have been uncovered. The older one (church EA) was larger and is thought to date from the middle of the fourth century, making it the oldest church discovered until now in western Anatolia. Its large size is interpreted as evidence for the existence of a large Christian community in Sardis. Although what has been excavated is in a

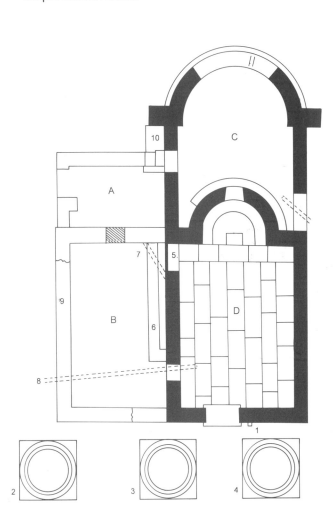

Marble relief cross from church E. Sardis.

very fragmentary condition it gives some idea of the general plan of the building; it consisted of a courtyard, narthex and nave with aisles. At present its eastern half is under the second church built on the same ground. The curved foundation of its apse with its supporting buttresses can be distinguished to the east side. However, the superstructure cannot be made out. Later, the building underwent various changes and constructions.

The second church (E) which was raised on the ruins of the previous one was smaller and dates from the Lascarid period. It was partly built out of surviving material of the previous building and occupied its eastern end. It consisted of a narthex and nave with side aisles. The apse, which was smaller than that of the previous church, can be distinguished. Its exterior was decorated with friezes of hollow quatrefoils made of clay pipes inserted vertically into the wall surface. Its fallen dome still survives at the centre of its ruins.

The five rectangular piers, preserved up to a height of ten metres and still partly buried in the field on the north side of the present highway, are thought to have belonged to the main church of Sardis (church D). It probably rose on the ground of an ancient temple. The piers were constructed with reused material and rubble with mortar and faced with irregular ashlar. Parts of pendentives and springing of sideways arches have survived. The building is thought to have continued to the north. Excavations are expected to give an idea about the plan of the building and about the person to whom it was dedicated.

(opposite) Ruins of churches E and EA in Sardis with the acropolis in the background (looking west). The remains of apses of both churches are distinguished in the foreground. The brickwork ruin at the centre is the dome of church E.

The Synagogue in Sardis

The Jewish community in Sardis is thought to possess a very early history. After the destruction of Jerusalem in 586 BCE the king of Babylon, Nebuchadnezzar, moved the king, his family, upper class citizens of the city, soldiers, scribes, priests and craftsmen to his capital (2 Kgs 24:10-16) where they stayed until its conquest by Cyrus the Great in 539 BCE. The next year Cyrus allowed the exiled Jews to return to Jerusalem and build the Second Temple. According to the book of Obadiah (Ob 20) which was written in the mid-fifth century BCE, when the Day of Judgement comes all the nations will be overhelmed and the Hebrews restored:

> And the captives of Jerusalem who
> are in Sepharad shall occupy the cit-
> ies of the Negeb.[1]

This shows that some of the Jerusalem refugees must have been exiled to Sepharad which is thought to be the name of Sardis in the Semitic language.

Also, the Seleucid king Antiochus III the Great (223-187 BCE) is said to have brought 2,000 loyal Jewish families from Babylonia and Mesopotamia and had them settle in Phrygia and Lydia. Since Sardis was the centre of Seleucid administration, it is very probable that some of the immigrants were settled here.

The synagogue in Sardis is the largest of its type known to date. Excavations show that the building was originally a civic basilica which was built between the main street and the gymnasium and converted into a synagogue sometime between 150-250. Its unusually large dimensions and rich decoration, as well as the titles of the Jews mentioned in the inscriptions here, show the high status that the Jewish community in Sardis held.

In its final form the synagogue which is thought to date from about 320-40 consisted of a colonnaded entrance court and a long assembly hall.

The forecourt was a peristyle paved with geometrical mosaics. The inscribed mosaic panels contain the names of donors such as 'Aurelius Polyppos, pious, having made a vow, I fulfilled it'. The corner columns of the portico

Reconstruction of the synagogue (A.M. Shapiro; revised by A.R. Seager).

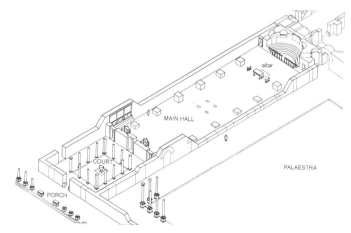

[1] The southern part of Judah

were heart-shaped and bore Ionic capitals. The walls of the courtyard were first decorated with plaster and later with marble revetments. It is probable that the courtyard was of two storeys to match the height of the main hall. The portico was separated from the open courtyard by a low balustrade which ran between the columns. Its centre had a marble fountain in the shape of a crater. It is thought that the forecourt was used as a gathering place before entering the main hall. The fountain served for the washing of hands before prayer. However it might have been a public fountain with the forecourt serving as a public centre.

The main hall, which is thought to have a capacity of nearly a thousand people begins with a pedimented shrine on either side of the entrance. These were probably used to deposit the scrolls of the Torah. At the other end there were the circular benches reserved for the 'elders' of the community. The large marble table which stands here is a unique feature and not encountered in any other synagogues. It was perhaps used to hold the Torah during readings. It is made of reused material the legs decorated with Roman eagles clutching thunderbolts. On either side of the table were pairs of marble lions of reused material from the Lydian period.[2]

The floor of the hall was covered with mosaics. An arched panel with an urn similar to the one in the forecourt, two peacocks and a vine scroll covered the floor in front at the apse. The walls were revetted with coloured marble. Their upper surface was probably covered with paintings and glass mosaics. The roof was supported by piers on either side.

The four pillars which stood at the centre of the hall were a later addition. The surviving part of the mosaic inscription shows that it was a donation of 'samoe, priest and sophodidas-kalos' (teacher of wisdom) and probably indicated the spot from where this teacher or rabbi taught. The four pillars probably supported a canopy over the mosaic.

[2] The original eagles and lions have been removed to Manisa Archaeological Museum.

Ruins of the Church of St John the Theologian in Philadelphia (looking north).

ANCIENT PHILADELPHIA

Philadelphia (Alaşehir) was founded by Attalos II Philadelphos[1] of Pergamum (159-138 BCE). The spot chosen for the new city was on the banks of the river Cogamus (Alaşehir Çayı) on the lower slopes of Mt Tmolus, controlling the routes converging in the area. In 481 BCE the Persian ruler Xerxes I had travelled by this route towards Sardis on his way to Greece. The objective of Attalos II in founding a city here was probably to establish a gateway to Phrygia and Hellenize its inhabitants who spoke their own Gallic tongue. When his nephew Attalos III, a weak and eccentric person, left the kingdom of Pergamum to Rome in 133 BCE, Philadelphia became Roman territory and was eventually part of the Byzantine Empire.

The region still grows some of the best grapes in Turkey and Philadelphia was famous for its wine. The god of

[1] In Greek 'loving one's brother or sister'; an epithet that he won because of the loyalty he had shown to his elder brother Eumenes II. The port he had established on the Pamphylian coast was also named Attalia (Antalya) after himself.

Marble pair of angels from Philadelphia. Byzantine period. Manisa Archaeological Museum.

wine was worshipped here under both his Greek and Latin names, Dionysus and Bacchus. The city must have been very prosperous during the Roman period because it was referred to as 'Little Athens'. In 17 it suffered a disastrous earthquake and was rebuilt by Tiberius who renamed it Neo-Caesarea.

Lacking natural defences the city was surrounded by a wall to protect it from Turkish raids. A section of this wall has survived on the north side. In 1391 it was captured by the Turks.

The church which has been named after St John was a rectangular building of six pillars of reused stone material and upper structure in brick. Three of its pillars have survived, with the fourth half buried in soil. The westernmost pillars are under modern buildings. On the pillars some eleventh-century paintings can barely be distinguished.

To the church in Philadelphia

To the angel of the church in Philadelphia, write this:
'The holy one, the true,
  who holds the key of David,
  who opens and no one shall close,
  who closes and no one shall open,
  says this:
''I know your works (behold, I have left an open door before you, which no one can close). You have limited strength, and yet you have kept my word and have not denied my name. Behold, I will make those of the assembly of Satan who claim to be Jews and are not, but are lying, behold I will make them come and fall prostrate at your feet, and they will realize that I love you. Because you have kept my message of endurance, I will keep you safe in the time of trial that is going to come to the whole world to test the inhabitants of the earth. I am coming quickly. Hold fast to what you have, so that no one may take your crown.

The victor I will make into a pillar in the temple of my God, and he will never leave it again. On him I will *inscribe the name of my God and the name of the city of my God, the new Jerusalem, which comes down out of heaven from my God, as well as my new name." '*

Whoever has ears ought to hear what the Spirit says to the churches.

(Rv 3:7-13)

Excepting Smyrna, Philadelphia is the only church among the seven about which nothing bad is said by St John. At the beginning of his letter to the members of the church in Philadelphia St John refers to Christ as the truth itself, and as the holder of the key of David. This is the key to open the holy city Jerusalem. These keys are referred to by God in Isaiah 22:22:

I will place the key of the House of David on his shoulder; when he opens, no one shall shut, when he shuts, no one shall open.

These are the keys of Death and Hades mentioned in the book of Revelation (Rv 1:18). They are access to the eschatological kingdom of God. The door's shutting means the irrevocable loss of the opportunity. The open door he has set before them is himself through whom they could enter the kingdom of heaven.

St John's words give the impression that the Christians in the church of Philadelphia are either small in number or poor or both; but they have not denied Christ. The Jews of Philadelphia are accused in the same way as the Jews of Smyrna, of being the 'assembly' of Satan: not true Jews but pretenders. These false Jews will come to the Christian Church and recognize that the Risen One loved the true believers, because the church of Philadelphia has followed the example of Christ's patient endurance.

Although they have little power the Christians of Philadelphia have kept Christ's word and if they keep to their faith they will be rewarded after the impending Second Coming. At the hour of trial Christ will stand by them. Among the promised rewards is that he who conquers will become a pillar in the temple of God and he shall never go out. The Greek word *stylos* means 'pillar' or 'support'. In both the Old and New Testaments it is often used both literally and metaphorically. The metaphor may refer to the two pillars which adorned Solomon's temple. In 1 Kings 7:21 and 2 Chronicles 3:17 Solomon sets up a pillar to the left of the entrance of his temple which he calls Boaz, and another one to the right named Yachin.[1]

The pillar bore three names: God, Jerusalem, and Christ. This is the final eschatological vision of St John in the book of Revelation and it describes the ultimate hope of the faithful which is a heavenly city. It will descend from heaven as the bride of the exalted Christ. Those who are marked as conquerors will be its citizens.

[1] The names are thought to mean '(God) established (the House) with might'.

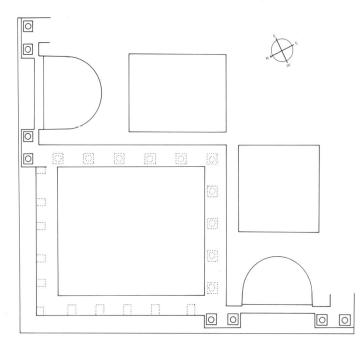

ANCIENT LAODICEA

Laodicea on the Lycus (Eskihisar) is thought to have been founded by the Seleucid King Antiochus II Theos (261-246 BCE) and named after his wife Laodice. The name of the river Lycus (Çürüksu) near which it was founded was attached to the name of the city to distinguish it from the other settlements of the same name.[1] The Lycus was a tributary of the river Meander whose water has been a major source of the region's agricultural wealth. As usual the spot chosen for the new city was on the most important trade and military route from the Aegean coast to the interior of Anatolia.

The objective of the Seleucid king was probably to es-

[1] His grandfather Seleucus I Nicator (321-280 BCE) had already founded five Laodiceas named after his own mother.

Plan of the Nymphaeum (after Bean).

(opposite) Ruins of the Nymphaeum which once served as a church in Laodicea.

tablish a stronghold on the main trade, communication and military route between the western coast and the hinterland against his northern enemy the Antigonids of Macedon.[2]

The early population of the city probably consisted of the natives of the area, Hellenized Greeks and veteran soldiers in the army of Antiochus II. After the battle of Magnesia (190 BCE) which the Seleucids lost against Rome, the region, including this city, was given to Eumenes II of Pergamum for his help in the battle. In 133 BCE in accordance with the will of Attalos III, the last king of Pergamum, Laodicea was incorporated in the Roman empire together with the rest of western Anatolia.

The population of the city must have included a Jewish community during the Roman period for it is known that in 62 BCE the Roman governor confiscated the annual sum that the Laodicean Jews had collected to be sent to the Temple in Jerusalem, for the public treasury. The evidence for the existence of a Jewish population is important because it was within such Jewish populations that the Christian religion found its first adherents. The great grandfathers of these Jews may have been some of those who were moved from the East and settled in the area by Antiochus III some two hundred years before. The famous Roman orator and statesman Cicero served as the governor of the province, residing mostly in Laodicea, in

[2] This route ran from Ephesus to the East. It was known as the 'common route' (koine hodos) and went through Tralles (Aydın), Laodicea, Apamea (Dinar), Antioch in Pisidia (Yalvaç) Philomelium (Akşehir), across Lycaonia to Iconium (Konya), Laranda (Karaman), through the Cilician Gates to Tarsus and finally to Antioch on the Orontes (Antakya) or across to Zeugma on the Euphrates.

known about the history of the city comes mostly from written sources. Zeus and Asclepius, whose cult was probably connected with the pre-Roman Anatolian moon-god Men, were the most popular deities. The city was known as an important medical centre, whose physicians specialized mostly in ear and eye complaints. The ointments against such diseases were shipped in tablet form all over the world. Wool was another source of wealth. According to the younger Pliny 'the country round Laodicea provides sheep that are excellent, not only for the softness of their wool, but also for its raven-black colour', it is not clear whether the black was the natural colour of the wool or obtained from a dye.

After the Roman period and the Byzantine era the city became battle ground for Byzantine armies, Turkish Emirates, the crusaders and Timurids and gradually fell into oblivion.

Preliminary excavations which revealed crosses at the ruins show that city had more than one church as early as the fifth century or probably earlier. One of these is thought to have stood near the so-called Syrian Gate.

A part of the early third-century nymphaeum is also thought to have been used as a church. This monument whose ruins stand at the centre of the city along a partly-excavated main street had been rebuilt several times in late antiquity and was abandoned in the seventh century after the Sassanian and Arab raids. The monuments consisted of a square water basin with colonnades on its inner sides flanked by smaller semicircular fountains which were supplied by the two chambers at the back and connected to the water tower by the gymnasium. The large basin was turned into a church.

51/50 BCE for about a year. In his letters he relates how badly the region was exploited both by the local officials and the previous Roman governors.

Although Laodicea received the generosity of the Roman emperors less than the rival coastal cities, it was founded on the network of trade routes and close to fresh water sources and flourished easily. Unfortunately, it was also founded on the major earthquake belt and natural disasters interrupted its progress and growth frequently. Strabo refers to these earthquakes by saying that the region is 'full of holes'. One of the most disastrous of such earthquakes occurred in 61 and devastated the whole area.

Once, when the Laodiceans were willing to erect a temple for Tiberius, their offer was turned down on the grounds that they could not meet the expense. However, the successors of Tiberius were more indulgent and in the time of Commodus (180-92) the city became a 'temple-keeper'. It shared the benefits of the economic and social boom brought by the Roman Peace and became a thriving urban centre.

Since almost no excavation has been done what is

So-called small theatre in Laodicea. The whiteness in the background is from the travertine formations of Hierapolis (Pamukkale).

Water-tower near the gymnasium. The terraccotta pipes show the thick layers of encrustation.

To the church in Laodicea

To the angel of the church in Laodicea, write this:

'The Amen, the faithful and true witness, the source of God's creation says this: "I know your works; I know that you are neither cold nor hot. I wish you were either cold or hot. So, because you are lukewarm, neither hot nor cold, I will spit you out of my mouth. For you say, 'I am rich and affluent and have no need of anything,' and yet do not realize that you are wretched, pitiable, poor, blind, and naked. I advise you to buy from me gold refined by fire so that you may be rich, and white garments to put on so that your shameful nakedness may not be exposed, and buy ointment to smear on your eyes so that you may see. Those whom I love, I reprove and chastise. Be earnest, therefore, and repent.

Behold, I stand at the door and knock. If anyone hears my voice and opens the door, (then) I will enter his house and dine with him, and he with me. I will give the victor the right to sit with me on my throne, as I myself first won the victory and sit with my Father on his throne.'

Whoever has ears ought to hear what the Spirit says to the churches.

(Rv 3:14-22)

In the opening words of his message St John introduces Christ as the 'Amen' which is His divine title. Christ is the true representation and the infallible witness of the glory of God and the firstborn or beginning of all creation.

St John does not accuse the church in Laodicea of apostasy. Neither does he charge them with following the teaching of a false prophet — worshipping the imperial cult. The Christians of Laodicea are accused of being 'lukewarm'. St John's play on the words 'cold, hot, lukewarm' shows that he is familiar with the rare luxury of the

Double-pipeline of stone blocks with encrustation. It brought water to Laodicea from the east.

region in respect to springs in the hot Anatolian summer. The metaphor is based on the water supply of Laodicea and water sources of nearby Hierapolis (Pamukkale) and Colossae (Honaz). The water which reached Laodicea after covering some seven kilometres by a pipe-line was so hard or impure that it caused thick layers of encrustation in the pipes which have survived among the ruins. According to St John it was almost too hard to swallow. The water of Hierapolis is hot whereas that of Colossae is cold. Being 'cold' or 'hot' for a beverage is preferable to being 'lukewarm'. The water of those cities is preferable to that of Laodicea.

St John's metaphor gives the impression that the rich church of Laodicea was unable to understand the real source of the richness of a church; what is the meaning of richness for a church? The Laodicean Christians are wealthy and self-content to a degree that they think that they do not need Christ. They are 'lukewarm' or 'slackened'. This is a pitiable condition. They could only become rich by turning to the Lord. They are poor because what they own is material. They are blind because they cannot see their obligations. They are naked because their clothes do not give them any spiritual warmth. They have neither refused the new faith nor embraced it strongly enough to provoke persecutions. This is not acceptable. Their peaceful happy life is nothing but an illusion. St John's remark that they buy *ointment to smear on*

your eyes so that you may see may derive from the fame of the eye medicine produced from powdered Phrygian stone in Laodicea. In a city famous for eye medicines the Christian church is blind.

St John informs them that in order to be rich in reality they must buy *gold refined by fire* that is the true Christian faith which will endure the test. Those who stand and die wear the *white garments* — contrasting the 'black wool' of the area — of a martyr. While the sought-after garment of Laodicea does not give anything but material warmth.

At the end of his message the vision describes the Risen Lord standing at the door knocking, and inviting those inside to open and receive him. The Lord is addressing the spiritually lukewarm church in Laodicea to open itself and let Him in. The door of eternal happiness is opened by obedience and faith. Thus they must repent and join, returning to Christ at the festal meal, an allusion deriving from Mark 14:25 and Luke 22:30 where Christ refers to a messianic banquet which he would celebrate with his disciples in the Heavenly Kingdom.

CONCLUSION

Tradition has it that when Noah saw that his ark was grounded on top of Mt Ararat and the flood water was receding he wished to celebrate it. Alas! There was nothing to cook. He collected what he found at the bottom of baskets and storage jars; fruits, nuts, grains and other scraps and cooked them together. The result was today's popular Turkish dish *aşure*, Noah's pudding. It is a sweet in which each of its ingredients retains its distinctive taste, yet the mixture has its own taste which is more than the total of all the tastes.

Compared to its limited size and resources Anatolia has been the home of a very unusual number and variety of cultures. It is a kind of *aşure* of cultures. The total of these cultures is more than their sum. Many archaeology students who visit the country fall in love with it and spend the rest of their lives uncovering its rich past; some even choose the sites they have dug as their graveyards.

The intercourse among these cultures, between their art, religion, script and language, was probably at its highest stage when St John left Palestine and travelled to Ephesus. The world in which he found himself was more cosmopolitan and perplexing than the Judaic world of Jerusalem. For a person to chose the right path was much more difficult than it is at present. Excavations which are being carried out bring to light more material than the archaeologists can handle. When this material is evaluated the role of Anatolia in the early growth of Christianity will be understood better.